Beyond Montague Island

Even More Mysteries and Logic Puzzles

R. Wayne Schmittberger

PUZZLE
WRIGHT
PRESS

New York

PUZZLE WRIGHT PRESS

New York

An Imprint of Sterling Publishing Co., Inc.
122 Fifth Avenue
New York, NY 10011

ISBN 978-1-4549-3659-6

Distributed in Canada by Sterling Publishing Co., Inc.
c/o Canadian Manda Group, 664 Annette Street
Toronto, Ontario M6S 2C8, Canada
Distributed in the United Kingdom by GMC Distribution Services
Castle Place, 166 High Street, Lewes, East Sussex BN7 1XU, England
Distributed in Australia by NewSouth Books
University of New South Wales, Sydney, NSW 2052, Australia

For information about custom editions, special sales, and premium and
corporate purchases, please contact Sterling Special Sales at 800-805-5489 or
specialsales@sterlingpublishing.com.

Manufactured in China

2 4 6 8 10 9 7 5 3 1

sterlingpublishing.com
puzzlewright.com

Cover image: Donnchans / Shutterstock.com

Contents

Introduction............4

Early Spring............5
Precautions • Toppings

Weekend 1............7
House Rules • Starting Out • The Purloined Necklaces • Menagerie

Weekend 2............12
Chez Thérèse • On Broadway • Double 9 Special • Alibis

Weekend 3............20
At the Sea Caves • Trivia Tic-Tac-Toe • Mansion Meanders • Footsteps

Interlude............25

Weekend 4............26
Weighted Voting • Murder in the Guest Wing • 1830 • 1856

Weekend 5............34
Major Arcana • Birdhouses • Wildflowers • Murder at the Lighthouse

Weekend 6............40
Amusement Park • Miniature Golf • Hard Candy

Weekend 7............46
Fantasy Chess Draft • Fantasy Chess Tournament • Seven, Zero • Around Midnight

Weekend 8............52
Who's Whose • Thrill Island Excursion • Paintball

Interlude............58

Weekend 9............59
Card-Jackers • Shady Shamuses • Curio Cabinet • All the Marbles

Interlude............63

Weekend 10............64
Bridge Pros • Bridge Amateurs • Knickknacks • Mental Blocks • Endgame

Late Summer............72
Arrangements

Answers and Explanations............74

Montague Island Map............11
Montague Mansion Floor Plan............23

Introduction

Welcome to my third *Montague Island* book. It's not necessary to have read the other books to enjoy this one, but only those who have read *Return to Montague Island* will have met Cheryl, who is now a main character.

Cheryl has just finished law school, and she and five of her law school classmates plan to spend the summer on Montague Island, first studying for their bar exams and then relaxing for a month before beginning their first jobs as attorneys. But an old enemy of Gordon Montague's has emerged as a possible threat, and so Gordon has once again asked for Taylor's help.

Taylor is an enigmatic person who seems to be a combination of private investigator, security consultant, and bodyguard. The books never reveal whether Taylor is male or female, but we do know Taylor is now about 48 years old.

My idea for these books was to tell a story set in a world in which mysteries and logic puzzles exist naturally, much like songs in a play whose subject is the making of a musical. And so I imagined an island home of a wealthy couple who are passionate about playing games, solving puzzles, and creating puzzles for others to solve. The Montagues regularly invite guests to their island to act out parts in mysteries that the Montagues have created, play in game tournaments, and solve a variety of puzzles.

For the first time in this series, some puzzles are not set on the island. The first and last puzzles take place in Ojai, California, and there are two weekends when most puzzles are based on events at a mainland amusement park not far from the island. Most of the time, however, you will find yourself in the familiar surroundings of the island's paths and Montague Mansion's many rooms and secret passages.

On a personal note, Gillespie is the maiden name of my maternal grandmother, who for many years lived a block from both Montague Street and Montague Terrace in Brooklyn Heights.

As usual the book includes some traditional logic puzzles that can be solved with a grid, unconventional puzzles that require special methods, and mysteries in which guilty suspects may make false statements to mislead the solver. My special thanks to Francis Heaney, whose puzzle-testing and editing have greatly improved both this and the previous two books.

May you enjoy your visit.

—R. Wayne Schmittberger

Precautions

You're at a well-appointed ranch-style home in Ojai, California, seated at a table in front of a picture window looking north toward tall mountains. Present are the homeowners Kirk and Linda Gillespie, their adult daughter Cheryl, their son Andrew, and Gordon and Nina Montague. Gordon is Linda's father.

"You've helped us before, and we're asking for your help again this summer," Gordon tells you. "We're not sure it's necessary, but we don't want to take any chances. Twenty years ago I exposed a prominent investment manager named Felix Hochstapler as a fraud, and he has been in prison ever since. At the end of May, his son, Felix Junior, who was convicted of lesser charges, will be released from prison.

"When the father was sent to prison, he vowed to get even with me one day. I don't know whether the son poses any kind of threat. The family has no history of violence, but they might try something sneaky, such as trying to frame me for a crime of some kind."

"It's the summer of my bar exam," Cheryl interjects. "Five of my law school classmates and I plan to spend the summer on Montague Island taking an online bar review course during the weekdays, hoping to have time for some games and puzzles on the weekends. Most of us will leave to take the exams in late July and then return to the island for a month's vacation before we begin our full-time jobs as lawyers. All of us have jobs lined up, starting in September, at the firms where we interned last summer."

Gordon continues: "Nina and I don't want Cheryl to be distracted by worries about Junior, so we'd like you to spend the summer on the island, as you have twice before, to keep an eye on things. Meanwhile, if there's a way you could have someone watch out for Linda and her family, we'd like you to arrange that too."

You already knew most of this when you agreed to come to Ojai, but you wanted to see the house to understand its security issues and meet Kirk, Linda, and Andrew. Cheryl and the Montagues, of course, you already knew well.

"I have a pair of operatives who would love to spend a summer in Ojai. There's a nearby house that is available for rent this summer, and they can watch your house from there with the help of some surveillance equipment they'll set up.

"So yes, I'd enjoy another summer on the island. It's a very secure place, but a clever and determined person still might find a way to cause you some kind of trouble."

"You'll find a few changes," Gordon says. "Last year a hurricane destroyed our boathouse and badly damaged our guest wing. It's a good thing we evacuated before the storm and got our cabin cruiser to the mainland and out of the water. We've rebuilt the boathouse as it was before, but we took the opportunity to redesign the guest wing. We reduced it from three floors to two, and made the rooms larger by having three rooms per floor instead of five. Since we don't have as many guests these days as we once did, and many of the ones we get are couples, it made sense. For convenience we also created second-floor access from the guest wing to the rest of the house by adding a hall that connects it to the existing second-floor hallway. We did, however, preserve the secret passage to the basement through the crawlspace. On the roof we added solar panels and a dish for satellite internet.

"Nolan still works for us part-time. He's often on the mainland, though lately he sometimes sleeps in the cabin cruiser. You can have your choice of staying in the cottage or one of the guest rooms in the mansion."

You plan to think that over as you try to imagine how you would go about getting revenge on Gordon Montague if you were in Junior's shoes.

Toppings

Before the Montagues, Cheryl, and Taylor fly back to the East Coast, everyone gets together for a meal. They order seven different personal-size pizzas. From the clues below, can you determine who had which pizza toppings?

1. Andrew, Cheryl, Gordon, Kirk, Linda, Nina, and Taylor each ordered three different toppings from the following vegetarian choices: artichokes, black olives, broccoli, mushrooms, onions, peppers, and spinach.

2. Each pizza topping was ordered by exactly three people, but no two people had more than one pizza topping in common.

3. Neither Andrew nor Taylor had either artichokes or onions.

4. Neither Gordon nor Kirk had either broccoli or mushrooms.

5. Neither Cheryl nor Nina had either black olives or peppers.

6. One of Kirk's toppings was also ordered by Andrew and Linda, and another of Kirk's toppings was ordered by Cheryl and Gordon.

7. Linda, who did not order onions, had a topping that was also ordered by Gordon and Nina.

8. One of Cheryl's toppings was also ordered by Linda and Taylor.

9. Andrew ordered mushrooms.

10. Linda did not order peppers.

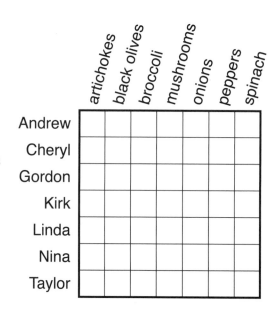

House Rules

On the Friday before Memorial Day weekend, you are standing on a pier on the South Carolina coast along with Cheryl and five of her law school classmates. She introduces you to Aria, Brianna, Danny, Kelly, and Steven. After the Montagues' cabin cruiser arrives, Alistair, the Montagues' head of staff, helps the guests bring their luggage aboard. All of them already know Nolan, the cabin cruiser's pilot whom Cheryl has been dating for three years. Montague Island, just a few miles offshore, is normally visible but today is shrouded in mist.

As the boat leaves shore, Cheryl addresses her classmates.

"As I've explained, Gordon and Nina Montague have a tradition of inviting summer guests to their island for weekends of playing games, solving puzzles, and sometimes acting out mysteries they have written. Even though we'll be busy with our bar review course, I'm hoping we'll find time for recreation on the weekends. And I'm glad that you will all be able to stay a couple more weeks after we take our bar exams.

"When there is a mystery to act out, you will become detectives whose goal is to solve the crime. At least one of you will be the person who committed the crime; but even if your character is guilty, you will not know this until you have solved the mystery like the other players. Before a mystery puzzle, you will be given a specific key statement that you are to make to other players when they question you. Such statements will always be true when spoken by an innocent character, but may or may not be true when spoken by a guilty party. You may embellish the phrasing of a key statement, provided you are careful not to change its essence.

"Everyone on the island prefers to go by their first name. That includes my grandfather Gordon, his wife Nina (who by the way is an attorney), Alistair, chef Evelyn, gardener Grant, nurse Lyle, secretary Charlotte, and housekeeper Sandy, all of whom live in the mansion. You will use your own first names in all mystery games, but other facts about you, such as your occupation or your favorite book, may be fictitious facts made up for purposes of a particular story.

"A prize will be awarded at the end of the summer to the guest who has been the first to correctly solve the most mystery puzzles, and so it will be important to get statements from everyone else as quickly as possible—statements from each of us, as well as from Gordon, Nina, and the staff members. When you question Gordon, Nina, or one of their staff, you can rely on their statements to be true. I, however, will be just another guest who could be guilty in a mystery. When you have a solution to a mystery, you may present it to Gordon, Nina, or any of their staff."

Aria asks, "Are you sure our phones will work on the island?"

"Yes," Cheryl replies, "almost anywhere, thanks to a cell tower on the mainland that is only about four miles away. And the mansion has Wi-Fi, although it's slower than you're probably used to."

Starting Out

Aria, Brianna, Cheryl, Danny, Kelly, and Steven graduated from the same law school this year. Last summer they interned at the law firms of Black & White, Cash & Carey, Dey & Knight, Hale & Hardy, Hart & Soul, and Hunt & Peck, not necessarily in that order, which are located in Atlanta, Chicago, Los Angeles, New York City, San Antonio, and Washington, D.C., also not necessarily in that order. Each of them has accepted an offer of a permanent position with the firm where they interned, starting in September.

From the following clues, can you determine which student interned at which firm, as well as the city in which each firm is located?

1. Aria, Brianna, and the student who interned at Hale & Hardy will be working in Atlanta, Chicago, and Los Angeles, not necessarily in that order.

2. Cheryl and the students who interned at Black & White and Dey & Knight will be working in New York City, San Antonio, and Washington, not necessarily in that order.

3. Danny and the students who interned at Hart & Soul and Hunt & Peck will be working in Chicago, New York, and Washington, not necessarily in that order.

4. Steven and the student who interned at Cash & Carey will be working in Atlanta and Los Angeles, in some combination.

5. Kelly interned in either Los Angeles or San Antonio.

6. Neither Dey & Knight nor Hart & Soul is in Washington.

7. Cheryl did not intern at Hunt & Peck.

8. Neither Brianna nor the student who interned at Cash & Carey will be working in Atlanta.

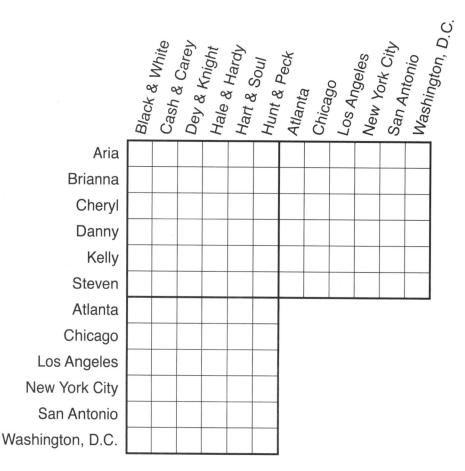

The Purloined Necklaces

The Montagues, their staff, and their guests (Aria, Brianna, Cheryl, Danny, Kelly, Steven, and Taylor) are playing roles as wealthy socialites who have gathered for a party at the mansion. Charlotte is playing the role of a relative of the Montagues who is currently their weekend guest. At 7 P.M., two valuable pieces of jewelry are discovered to be missing. Can you determine the identity of the thief or thieves?

Statements by the Montagues:

1. Gordon: Two valuable necklaces were stolen tonight between 6 and 7 P.M. They had been left out in plain view, one in the master bedroom on the third floor and the other in a second floor staff room where Charlotte has been staying.

2. Nina: My diamond necklace disappeared from my room, which I don't keep locked, between 6 and 7 P.M. As usual in our mysteries, only a guilty party may make a false statement.

Statements by the staff:

3. Alistair: There were not more than two thieves, and if there were two, they may have been working independently.

4. Charlotte: I'm a cousin of the Montagues staying in room on the second floor of the staff wing. My pearl necklace disappeared from my room, which I don't keep locked, between 6 and 7 P.M.

5. Evelyn: Only one of the guests went to the third floor between 6 and 7 P.M.

6. Grant: Danny could not have stolen anything between 6 and 6:30.

7. Lyle: Taylor could not have stolen anything between 6:30 and 7.

8. Sandy: Only one of the guests went to the second floor of the staff wing between 6 and 7 P.M.

Statements by the guests:

9. Aria: Kelly never left the first floor between 6 and 7.

10. Brianna: Aria never left the first floor between 6 and 7. Taylor could not have stolen anything between 6 and 6:30.

11. Cheryl: I saw Steven coming down the stairs from the third floor around 6:30.

12. Danny: I saw either Aria or Cheryl enter the second floor of the staff wing around 6:30.

13. Kelly: Brianna never left the first floor between 6 and 7 P.M. Danny could not have stolen anything between 6:30 and 7.

14. Steven: I was never on the third floor or on the stairs that go there.

15. Taylor: I saw either Danny or Steven go up to the second floor and enter either the staff wing or the stairs to the third floor.

Menagerie

On a recent trip to California, the Montagues discovered an artist who uses a chainsaw to carve large animal figures out of large pieces of wood. The sculptures are suitable for placing outdoors. The Montagues ordered 10 different animal sculptures (bear, cougar, deer, eagle, fox, groundhog, otter, raccoon, tortoise, and wolf) and shipped them to Montague Island, where they have now been placed at 10 different locations (boathouse, bridge, lighthouse, Lookout Point, mansion, old hut, old well, pond, sea caves, and windmill).

From the clues below, can you determine the location of each animal sculpture? Within the clues, distances are measured by the number of five-minute time intervals that it takes to walk from one location to another by the shortest route along the island's paths. These time intervals are shown in the table below.

1. The cougar, fox, and raccoon sculptures are at locations farther north than the mansion.

2. The eagle, groundhog, and tortoise sculptures are at locations farther east than the old well.

3. Of the bear, deer, otter, and wolf sculptures, the deer and otter are the closest together.

4. The eagle is the same distance from the otter and the fox.

5. The raccoon is the same distance from the eagle and the wolf.

6. The cougar is the same distance from the deer and the tortoise.

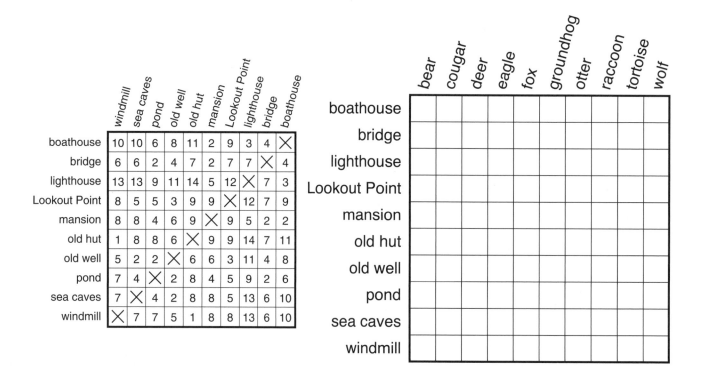

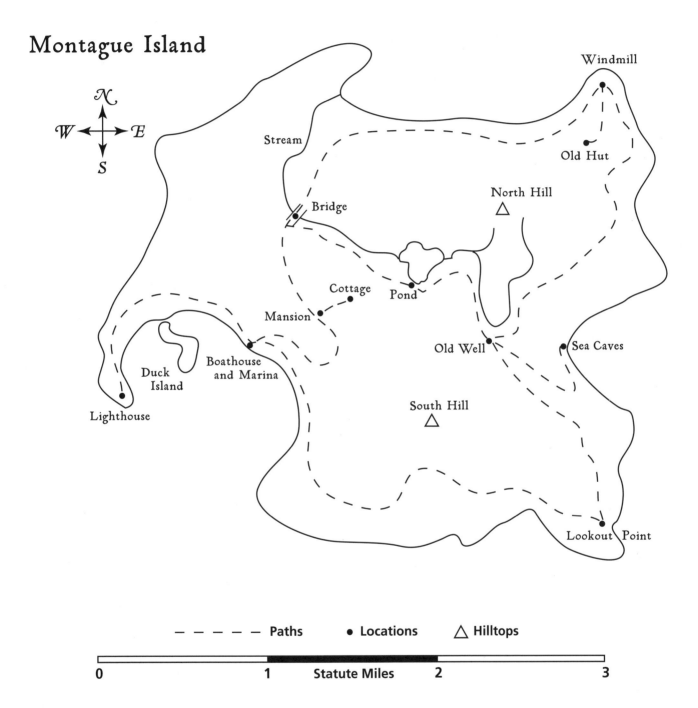

Montague Island

Windmill

Stream

Old Hut

North Hill

Bridge

Pond

Cottage

Mansion

Old Well

Sea Caves

Duck Island

Boathouse and Marina

South Hill

Lighthouse

Lookout Point

– – – – – Paths • Locations △ Hilltops

0 — 1 — Statute Miles — 2 — 3

Chez Thérèse

Rarely do the Montagues eat in restaurants unless they are traveling, since Evelyn is an avid and superb chef. In celebration of all the guests having finished law school, however, Gordon and Nina invite the guests and Nolan to Chez Thérèse, a fine French restaurant that is within walking distance of the mainland pier where they normally dock their cabin cruiser. From the clues below, can you determine who ordered what menu items for each of the four courses?

1. The restaurant party ended up ordering a total of four different hors d'oeuvres (avocado cocktail, chef's mussels, escargots, hearts of palm), four different salads or soups (beet salad, Caesar salad, French onion soup, soup du jour), four different main courses (filet mignon, gnocchi champignons, poulet à la lavande, saumon à l'orange), and four different desserts (cheesecake, chocolate mousse, crème brûlée, opera torte).

2. In each of the four courses (hors d'oeuvre, soup or salad, main course, dessert), one item was ordered by four people, one item was ordered by three people, one item was ordered by two people, and one item was ordered by just one person.

3. Aria, Cheryl, Danny, and Nolan each ordered one item that no one else ordered, one item that just one other person ordered, one item that two other people ordered, and one item that three other people ordered. Of the four, only Danny did not have avocado cocktail.

4. Only Aria, Danny, and Taylor ate filet mignon or saumon à l'orange.

5. Aria, Gordon, Kelly, Nolan, and Taylor ordered beet salad or Caesar salad, and everyone else ordered French onion soup or the soup du jour.

6. Every item Nina ordered was ordered by three other people.

7. Every item Kelly ordered was ordered by exactly two other people.

8. Brianna and Steven ordered all the same items.

9. Four people's orders included both gnocchi champignons and crème brûlée, and three of those people also had the soup du jour.

10. Brianna and Kelly had the same hors d'oeuvre, Gordon and Taylor had the same hors d'oeuvre, and only one person ordered chef's mussels.

11. Aria and Cheryl both had chocolate mousse.

12. Kelly and Gordon ordered different main courses.

13. Two people's orders included both hearts of palm and the soup du jour, and more people ordered hearts of palm than beet salad.

14. Two people's orders included both Caesar salad and cheesecake.

15. Two people's orders included both saumon à l'orange and cheesecake.

On Broadway

The Montagues want to add five more songs to their playlist of Broadway show tunes. With hundreds of well-known songs to choose from, they've selected 10 that are not currently on their list—"Aquarius," "Cabaret," "If I Loved You," "Mame," "Maria," "Memory," "Ol' Man River," "People," "Tomorrow," and "Tonight"—and have asked the seven guests (Aria, Brianna, Cheryl, Danny, Kelly, Steven, and Taylor) to each pick their five favorites from the list of 10. The Montagues will then add the five songs that appear on the most lists to their playlist. From the clues below, can you determine which songs are on each guest's list?

1. Each guest's lists contains five songs. One song is on six of the seven guests' lists, two songs each are on two, three, four, and five lists, and one song is on just one list.

2. "Cabaret" appears on more lists than "Maria," which appears on more lists than "Tomorrow," which appears on more lists than "If I Loved You." "Memory" appears on more lists than "Tonight," which appears on more lists than "People," which appears on more lists than "Ol' Man River."

3. "Aquarius" and "Mame" are on the same number of lists.

4. Neither "If I Loved You" nor "Mame" is on the lists of Aria, Brianna, Cheryl, or Danny.

5. Neither Brianna's list nor Cheryl's list includes "Aquarius" or "Ol' Man River."

6. Neither Danny's list nor Taylor's list includes "Tomorrow" or "Tonight."

7. Neither Kelly's list nor Steven's list includes "Cabaret," "Ol' Man River," or "People."

8. Of "Maria" and "Memory," one appears on Danny's list but not Kelly's, and the other appears on Kelly's list but not Danny's.

9. Of "Aquarius" and "Maria," one appears on Steven's list but not on Taylor's, and one appears on Taylor's list but not Steven's.

10. Of "People" and "Tomorrow," one appears on Aria's list but not Brianna's, and one appears on Brianna's list but not Aria's.

11. Only one song is on both Aria's and Kelly's lists.

12. Exactly four songs appear on the lists of both Brianna and Steven.

13. "Tomorrow" appears on fewer lists than "Aquarius."

	"Aquarius"	"Cabaret"	"If I Loved You"	"Mame"	"Maria"	"Memory"	"Ol' Man River"	"People"	"Tomorrow"	"Tonight"
Aria										
Brianna										
Cheryl										
Danny										
Kelly										
Steven										
Taylor										
1										
2										
3										
4										
5										
6										

Number of Lists

Double 9 Special

Taylor has devised a new way to play poker with dominoes. Unlike most previous versions of domino poker, in which doubles (double blank, double 1, etc.) are treated as a separate suit, Taylor's game requires removing all the doubles from a double-9 set before playing. That leaves 45 tiles, each having pips representing a unique combination of two numbers ranging from 0 through 9.

Each hand consists of five dominoes, and a player gets to choose which half of each domino to use to form a five-number hand. The player indicates which halves are being used by placing the active halves toward the center of the table.

There is one exception: A "Special" hand consists of five dominoes whose halves contain all possible pip counts from 0 through 9, like this:

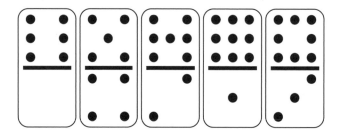

This is the highest possible hand. Other hands rank as in poker, although there are no flushes or straight flushes (see the box at right).

Taylor has made up the following puzzle based on the game. Five players (A, B, C, D, and E) have the sets of three dominoes shown on the next page. Two of three other dominoes, labeled X, Y, and Z, will be turned up to be a fourth and fifth domino shared by all the players to complete their hands.

Here is how the hands would rank if tiles X and Y, X and Z, or Y and Z were everyone's fourth and fifth tiles. Can you identify the numbers of pips on dominoes X, Y, and Z?

With tiles X and Y added, the hands rank from highest to lowest A, C, E, B, D.

With tiles X and Z added, the hands rank from highest to lowest B, C, D, E, A.

With tiles Y and Z added, the hands rank from highest to lowest E, B, A, C, D.

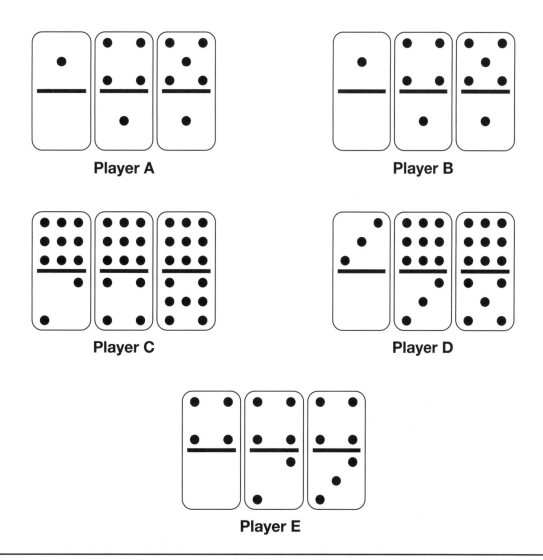

Player A

Player B

Player C

Player D

Player E

Ranks of Hands in Double-9 Special (highest to lowest)

Special: five dominoes that together show every number of pips from 0 through 9

five of a kind: five half-dominoes with the same number of pips, such as 4-4-4-4-4

four of a kind: four half-dominoes with the same number of pips, such as 5-5-5-5 plus any fifth half domino

full house: three half-dominoes with the same number of pips, plus two other half dominoes with the same number of pips, such as 1-1-1-6-6

straight: five half-dominoes whose number of pips forms a sequence, such as 8-7-6-5-4

three of a kind: three half-dominoes with the same number of pips, plus two other half-dominoes

two pair: two half-dominoes with the same number of pips, and two other half-dominoes with the same number of pips

pair: one pair of half-dominoes with the same number of pips

There is no "nothing" hand, because a player with no pairs has a Special.

In comparing hands that both have five of a kind, four of a kind, three of a kind, or a pair, the higher hand wins (e.g., five 8's beats five 7's). In comparing full houses, the higher-ranking three of a kind wins over the lower ranking three of a kind, and the pairs only are compared if both players have the same three of a kind. In comparing straights, the highest card in a hand wins. In comparing hands with two pairs, the hand with the higher-ranking pair wins.

Alibis

In this murder mystery written by the Montagues, who are currently traveling, the guests are playing cousins whose uncles Barney and Charlie had come to the island for the weekend. The guests have seven different occupations: actuary, beekeeper, clerk, designer, electrician, financier, and geologist.

After a second death in two days is discovered Sunday afternoon, the staff and guests meet in the lounge. From everyone's statements, can you match each guest to his or her occupation and determine who's responsible for the death of the two uncles?

Statements by the staff:

1. Alistair: Yesterday Uncle Barney's body was found floating in the pond at 5 p.m., two hours after he had left the mansion to take a walk. It first appeared that he had slipped near the edge of the pond and hit his head on a rock as he fell into the water. Later examination revealed he had received a blow to the head from behind, so he was actually murdered. As usual, only the guilty party or parties may make a false statement.

2. Charlotte: On Friday night, the cousins and their uncles had a lively discussion about wills and inheritances. Barney intended to leave all his wealth to Charlie unless Charlie died first, in which case Barney would leave everything to charity. Charlie intended to leave everything to Barney unless Barney died first, in which case Charlie would leave everything to his nephews and nieces (the cousins).

3. Evelyn: At 4 p.m. today I found Uncle Charlie dead in the second-floor hallway near the private study, at the foot of the stairs leading up to the special guest rooms on the third floor. I thought he had fallen or had a medical emergency until I discovered a wound on the back of his head that could only have been caused by being struck by a hard object.

4. Grant: Uncle Charlie was alive and well at 1 p.m. this afternoon, when he said he was going to spend some time reading in his third-floor special guest room.

5. Lyle: There were two killers, who were never together on Sunday between 1 p.m. and 4 p.m. Neither killer lies about having spent time with any specific individual (whether specifying them by name or occupation).

6. Sandy: On Sunday two guests each spent an hour in the library: Danny from 1 p.m. to 2 p.m. and Brianna from 3 p.m. to 4 p.m.

Statements by the guests:

7. Aria: From 3 p.m. until 5 p.m. yesterday I was alone in my room in the guest wing. From 1 p.m. until 2 p.m. today I took a walk around the island along with the clerk and the beekeeper. From 2 p.m. until 3 p.m., I took a walk with the actuary and the financier. From 3 p.m. until 4 p.m., I took a walk with the two guests I had not yet taken a walk with.

8. Brianna: From 3 p.m. until 5 p.m. yesterday I was alone in my room in the guest wing. From 1 p.m. until 2 p.m. today I took a walk around the island along with Steven and the geologist. From 2 p.m. until 3 p.m., I took a walk with the actuary and the designer.

9. Cheryl: From 3 P.M. until 5 P.M. yesterday I was alone in my room in the guest wing. From 1 P.M. until 2 P.M. today I took a walk around the island along with Aria and the beekeeper. From 2 P.M. until 3 P.M., I took a walk with two other guests. From 3 P.M. until 4 P.M., I was in the lounge with Kelly and another guest.

10. Danny: From 3 P.M. until 5 P.M. yesterday I was playing a game of Clue in the small game room with the electrician, geologist, and one other guest. On Sunday from 2 P.M. until 3 P.M., I took a walk around the island with Aria and one other guest. From 3 P.M. until 4 P.M., I was in the lounge with Cheryl and another guest.

11. Kelly: From 3 P.M. until 5 P.M. yesterday I was playing a game of Clue in the small game room with Danny and two other guests. From 1 P.M. until 2 P.M. today I took a walk around the island along with the designer and one other guest. From 2 P.M. until 3 P.M., I took a walk with two other guests. From 3 P.M. until 4 P.M., I was in the lounge with the actuary and one other guest.

12. Steven: From 1 P.M. until 2 P.M. today I took a walk around the island along with two other guests. From 2 P.M. until 3 P.M., I took a walk with two guests, one of whom was the clerk. From 3 P.M. until 4 P.M., I took a walk with two guests, one of whom I was also with the previous hour.

13. Taylor: From 3 P.M. until 5 P.M. yesterday I was playing a game of Clue in the small game room with Steven and two other guests. From 1 P.M. until 2 P.M. today I took a walk around the island along with Steven and one other guest. From 2 P.M. until 3 P.M., I took a walk with Steven and a different other guest. From 3 P.M. until 4 P.M., I took a walk with two guests, one of whom I had walked with the previous hour.

	Sat. 3–5	Sun. 1–2	Sun. 2–3	Sun. 3–4	actuary	beekeeper	clerk	designer	electrician	financier	geologist
Aria											
Brianna											
Cheryl											
Danny											
Kelly											
Steven											
Taylor											
actuary											
beekeeper											
clerk											
designer											
electrician											
financier											
geologist											

At the Sea Caves

"The sea caves on the eastern coast of Montague Island have three entrances, which I call A, B, and C from left to right as viewed from offshore," Gordon says to the guests. "I've hidden a prize in one of them, which can be retrieved by walking into the cave at low tide. The winner of the prize will be the person who is the first to correctly answer all the following questions and identify the location of the prize.

"The questions involve sets of three signs that might be placed at the three cave entrances and which may contain true or false statements. From the signs' content and the information provided about how many of the signs' statements are true or false, determine the location of the prize in each instance. Then the true location will be the one (of caves A, B, and C) that is the least common answer to the eight questions."

CAVE A	CAVE B	CAVE C
The prize is not here.	The prize is not in Cave A.	The prize is not here.

1. Where is the prize if all three of the above statements are true?
2. Where is the prize if only two of the above statements are true?
3. Where is the prize if only one of the above statements is true?

CAVE A	CAVE B	CAVE C
The prize is not in Cave C.	The prize is here or in Cave C.	The prize is not in Cave A.

4. Where is the prize if all three of the above statements are true?
5. Where is the prize if only two of the above statements are true?
6. Where is the prize if only one of the above statements is true?

CAVE A	CAVE B	CAVE C
The statement at Cave C is false.	The prize is here.	The statement at Cave B is false.

7. Where is the prize if it is in the cave that makes the greatest number of these three statements true?

CAVE A	CAVE B	CAVE C
The statements at Caves B and C are both false.	The prize is in Cave A.	The prize is not in Cave B.

8. The prize is in the cave that can definitively be identified by knowing how many of these three statements are true. Where is it?

Trivia Tic-Tac-Toe

Taylor has devised a new version of tic-tac-toe in which trivia questions must be answered to capture a square and place an X or O in it. Index cards, each containing one trivia question, are stacked on the squares of a large tic-tac-toe grid: four on the center square, three on each corner square, and two on each of the other four squares. (The number of cards corresponds to the number of different winning three-in-a-row lines that can be made through each square.) Besides the 24 questions stacked on the board, Taylor has written some additional questions that may be needed during the game.

The other six guests are divided into two teams of three. Each team's members must take turns answering questions throughout the game—that is, the order of answering within a team must be player A, player B, player C, player A, player B, etc.

A straight line of three X's or O's (horizontally, vertically, or diagonally) wins the game for the X or O team, respectively. If neither team achieves a three-in-a-row, the questions on the final square(s) are answered, and the team with more correct answers throughout the course of the game wins.

X goes first. Teams take a turn by choosing a square and answering the top trivia question there. If correct, the next player on the team answers the next question on the same square. If they reach the last trivia question on a square and answer it correctly, the square is captured and an X or O is put there. If a player answers a question incorrectly, that question is discarded and play passes to the other team, which answers the next question on the same square. If the last question on a square is answered incorrectly, a new question is placed there from Taylor's reserve questions. Thus, to capture a square, it is always necessary to answer the last question on that square correctly. Answering the final question correctly and capturing the square ends that team's turn, no matter who originally chose the square.

A closely contested game ensued, resulting in the diagram shown. The number in each square shows the order in which an X or O was placed there. From the clues below, can you determine who was on each team and which team won?

1. The X team began by answering a question incorrectly, but X won the first square anyway.
2. Aria gave fewer correct answers than Cheryl.
3. Brianna captured two squares for her team by answering the last question on those squares correctly.
4. Danny answered two more questions correctly than incorrectly.
5. Each of Kelly's correct answers captured a square.
6. Steven gave the fewest correct answers.
7. Each team answered a total of 14 questions.
8. Five questions on the center square were answered, more than on any other square.
9. The three players on the O team had the following in common: Three questions were answered by others between each one's first and second questions, and six questions were answered by others between each one's second and third questions.
10. Four questions were answered on the final square.

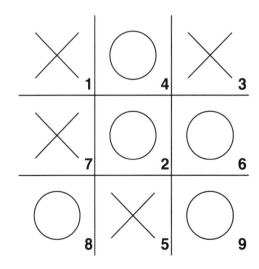

Mansion Meanders

A few minutes before a planned rendezvous in the sitting room on the second floor, the seven guests are scattered around the mansion. As previously agreed when they synchronized their watches, the guests all leave for the sitting room at the same time. They take the fastest possible routes to the sitting room, given the following condition: Guests must spend a full minute in each new room, hallway, stairway, closet, storage area, secret passage, or tunnel they enter.

All the secret passages and the doors between the tunnels and basement 2 are unlocked. A secret passage may be entered from any adjacent closet, storage room, or tunnel, and may be left by entering any adjacent closet, storage room, or tunnel, which may be on any floor directly above or below the floor where the passage was entered. All but one of the secret passages (the one that connects the two closets between the two basements) have ladders.

For example, a guest could go from the foyer on the first floor to one of the adjacent closets, then to the secret passage (labeled "Crw" for crawlspace on the floor plan), and from there could exit in any of the following: the storage area off basement 1, the closet off the sitting room closet, the closet next to the bath off the small game room, or the closet off the master bedroom. (This secret passage is split in two on the first and second floors, but the halves connect in both the basement and on the third floor.) Under the agreed rules, a guest taking such a trip would spend one minute in the closet, one minute in the secret passage, and one minute in the closet or storage area where the person exits (no matter which floor it's on). Going from the foyer to the sitting room this way would take three minutes between rooms. However, taking the stairs from the foyer to the second-floor hallway and then going to the sitting room would take only two minutes (one for the stairs, one for the hallway).

The stairs in the foyer connect to the foyer as well as to both the first- and second-floor hallways; the landing on the foyer stairway does not count as a separate room or stairway. No matter how far a person travels within a hallway, only one minute is spent there.

From the following clues, can you determine which guest started where?

1. Each guest begins in a different one of the following rooms (shaded on the blueprint at right): basement 2, big game room, game alcove, guest room 1A, library, master bath, wine cellar.

2. Aria, Danny, and Steven, only one of whom used a secret passage, all took the same amount of time to reach the sitting room.

3. Aria began higher up than Danny but below Steven's floor.

4. Taylor reached the sitting room faster than Cheryl, who reached it faster than Kelly, who despite not taking the foyer stairs reached it faster than Brianna, who never entered the guest wing.

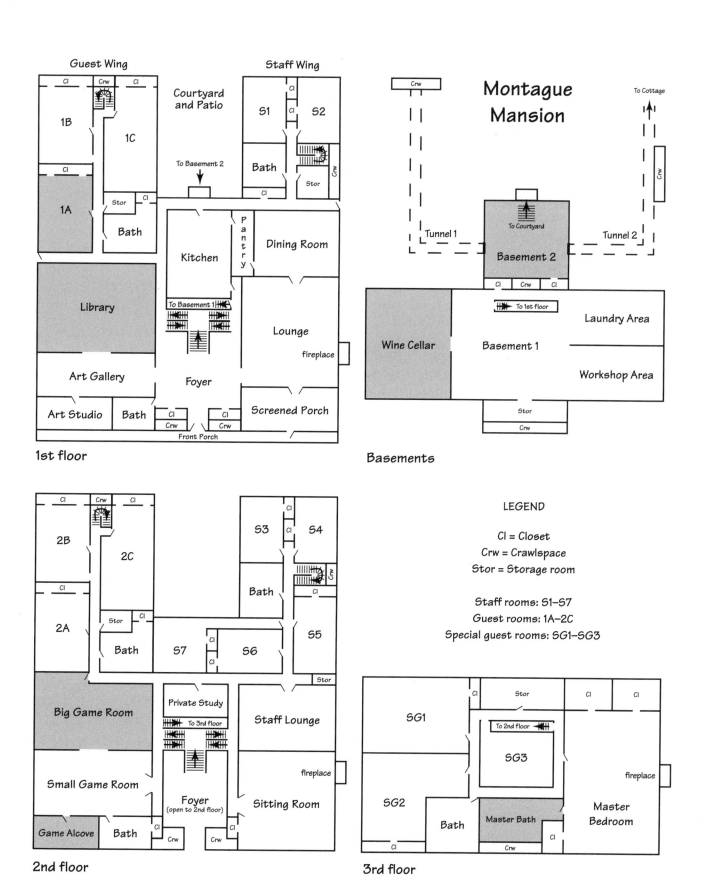

Guest Wing

Staff Wing

Cl | Crw | Cl

1B

1C

Courtyard and Patio

To Basement 2

Cl

S1 | S2

Bath

Stor

Crw

Cl

1A

Stor

Cl

Bath

Pantry

Kitchen

Dining Room

To Basement 1

Lounge

Library

fireplace

Art Gallery

Foyer

Art Studio | Bath

Cl | Crw

Cl | Crw

Screened Porch

Front Porch

1st floor

Montague Mansion

Crw

To Cottage

Crw

Tunnel 1

To Courtyard

Basement 2

Tunnel 2

Cl | Crw | Cl

To 1st floor

Laundry Area

Wine Cellar

Basement 1

Workshop Area

Stor

Crw

Basements

Cl | Crw | Cl

2B

2C

S3 | S4

Cl

Bath

Cl

2A

Stor | Cl

S5

Bath

S7 | S6

Cl
Cl

Stor

Big Game Room

Private Study

To 3rd floor

Staff Lounge

Small Game Room

Foyer
(open to 2nd floor)

fireplace

Game Alcove | Bath

Cl | Crw

Crw

Sitting Room

2nd floor

LEGEND

Cl = Closet
Crw = Crawlspace
Stor = Storage room

Staff rooms: S1–S7
Guest rooms: 1A–2C
Special guest rooms: SG1–SG3

Cl | Stor | Cl | Cl

SG1

To 2nd floor

SG3

fireplace

SG2

Bath | Master Bath | Cl

Cl | Crw

Master Bedroom

3rd floor

Footsteps

In this murder mystery, the guests are portraying members of the Atlantic Art Appreciation Association, a small group of wealthy art collectors and enthusiasts who meet irregularly to discuss their recent and planned future acquisitions. This weekend's gathering at Montague Island is interrupted when one of the members is found dead late Saturday morning. From the statements of the Montagues, staff, and guests, can you identify the killer?

Statements by the Montagues:

1. Gordon: Shortly after 11 A.M. I found the victim, played by Nolan, who had been stabbed to death in the private study on the second floor. The murder could have been accomplished in less than a minute. The victim had discovered that another member of the Association had knowingly acquired a stolen painting and threatened to inform the authorities.

2. Nina: The murder occurred between 10 A.M. and 11 A.M. During that hour, neither Gordon nor I used any stairs. None of the guests lie about where they were at 10 A.M. or at 11 A.M., and none of them except the killer fail to mention any of their movements around the mansion. There was only one killer, and only the killer may give a false statement.

Statements by the staff:

3. Alistair: None of the staff members used any stairs between 10 A.M. and 11 A.M. In moving from one mansion floor to another, each guest took less than five minutes, and no two guests were ever moving around the mansion at the same time. Any guest who used the foyer stairs more than once did so without any other guest using the foyer stairs in between.

4. Charlotte: I was in the second-floor hall a few minutes after 10 A.M. and saw Cheryl leave the big game room and head toward the foyer stairs about five minutes before Taylor left guest room 2A.

5. Evelyn: Between 10 A.M. and 11 A.M., I was in staff room S1, where it's not possible to hear anyone on the foyer stairs. But I went to the pantry twice during that hour. The first time, I heard two people in a row coming down the foyer stairs about five minutes apart from one another. The second time I again heard two people in a row coming down the stairs, this time about 10 minutes apart from one another.

6. Grant: I was in the dining room from about 10:50 A.M. to 11 A.M. During that time I heard two people go up the foyer stairs, about five minutes apart, and no one came down the stairs.

7. Lyle: Between 10 A.M. and 11 A.M., no guests used a secret passage, and neither of the two guests who used the guest wing stairs used the foyer stairs. Anyone in guest room 1B, 1C, 2B, or 2C can hear someone go up or down the guest wing stairs.

8. Sandy: I was in the staff lounge from 10 A.M. until 11 A.M., and I heard people going up or down the foyer stairs a total of nine times.

Statements by the guests:

9. Aria: I was in the library at 10 A.M., as was Steven. I heard people going up or down the foyer stairs five times, not more than five minutes apart from one another, before I went upstairs to the sitting room. Soon after I got to the sitting room I realized I had forgotten a book I meant to bring upstairs, so I went back down to get it and brought it back up to the sitting room.

10. Brianna: At 10 A.M. I was in guest room 2B. Sometime later I heard someone take the guest wing stairs up to the second floor. About 10 minutes later I went down the guest wing stairs and walked to the lounge, where I found Kelly and Taylor. We all stayed there until after 11 A.M. While there I heard people go up or down the foyer stairs four times.

11. Cheryl: At 10 A.M. I was in the big game room, as was Kelly. Sometime later I took the foyer stairs down and went to guest room 1A, where I was at 11 A.M.

12. Danny: I was in the art gallery from 10 A.M. until almost 11 A.M., when I climbed the foyer stairs and went to the small game room. I heard some people on the foyer stairs before I used them, but I didn't pay attention to whether they were going up or down.

13. Kelly: I was in the big game room with Cheryl at 10 A.M. Sometime after she left, I went down the foyer stairs to the lounge, where Brianna soon joined me. Taylor was already there.

14. Steven: I was in the library at 10 A.M., as was Aria. I heard someone on the foyer stairs four times, just a few minutes apart. After that I left the library and took the guest wing stairs up to guest room 2C, where I was at 11 A.M. When I left the library, Aria was still in it.

15. Taylor: I was in guest room 2A at 10 A.M. Sometime later I took the foyer stairs down and went to the lounge, where I remained until 11 A.M. Kelly and Brianna soon joined me there.

Between Weekends 3 and 4   **Interlude**

You update Gordon on your investigation so far. "From talking to the prison warden and running checks on Junior's closest prison acquaintances, we determined that even before getting out of prison, he enlisted the help of a recently released inmate. Junior was just an accomplice in his father's white-collar crime and didn't have outside criminal contacts, but in prison he met someone named Aiden Kreuk, who for a fee would perform all sorts of illegal activities. And since Junior has access to concealed off-shore bank accounts, he was able to promise payment to Kreuk.

"I'm sure now that the Hochstaplers know of your relation to Cheryl. It took some time to learn of Kreuk and track his movements. After being released from prison in late March, he went to the Raleigh area, and we suspect that he began to look for someone who could get close enough to Cheryl to get an invitation to the island.

"We're confident that the regular guests who have been her law school classmates for three years are all trustworthy, but she may have met other people who are not. Or Kreuk might have tried to find an unscrupulous contractor working for you, perhaps on a painting or repair project, who would be willing to do something illegal. We all need to stay on high alert whenever anyone new is on the island. I plan to share all this with Cheryl and Nolan, but I see no need to worry the other guests just yet.

"Since Junior was released, we've been following him as well, but he has been traveling around a lot and often goes to places where he could meet someone without our seeing."

Weighted Voting

The seven guests held a vote to choose a TV series to watch from the 10 suggested by the Montagues: *Bestworld*, *Big Little Pies*, *Boardwalk Umpire*, *Breaking Bald*, *Counterparty*, *Game of Clones*, *Masters of Hex*, *Outlandish*, *Truly Bloody*, and *Twin Beaks*.

Each guest had six poker chips to cast as votes as follows among three different shows: three chips for their first choice, two chips for their second choice, and one chip for their third choice.

Guests were awarded points equal to the sum of the number of all chips received by the three shows they voted for.

From the clues, can you determine which shows received how many chips from each guest, the total number of chips received by each show, and the number of points earned by each guest?

1. Every show received at least one chip, and the most chips any show received was 10.

2. The shows all ended up with a different number of chips except for three shows that each received just 1 chip.

3. Aria and Brianna voted for *Twin Beaks*.

4. Brianna and Taylor gave the same number of chips to one of the shows.

5. Brianna's point total was higher than Danny's but one less than Cheryl's.

6. Cheryl gave 3 chips to *Game of Clones* and also voted for *Breaking Bald* and *Outlandish*.

7. Danny's single-chip vote for *Big Little Pies* and Steven's single-chip vote for *Counterparty* were the only votes those shows received.

8. Danny voted for *Bestworld* and *Game of Clones* and ended up with 19 points.

9. Kelly voted for the show that received 4 chips, and no one else who voted for that show gave it the same number of chips that she did.

10. Steven voted for the show that received 3 chips.

11. Taylor voted for the three shows that received the most chips, which included *Outlandish*.

12. *Boardwalk Umpire*, *Breaking Bald*, *Truly Bloody*, and *Twin Beaks* received 1, 2, 3, and 4 chips, in some combination, and *Boardwalk Umpire* received more chips than *Twin Beaks*.

13. *Bestworld* and *Game of Clones* each got votes from four different guests, more guests than voted for any other shows.

14. Three of the guests had point totals of 10, 12, and 14.

15. No show received 3 chips from more than two different guests.

	Aria	Brianna	Cheryl	Danny	Kelly	Steven	Taylor	Sets of 3 chips	Pairs of chips	Single chips	Total chips
Bestworld	3 2 1 0	3 2 1 0	3 2 1 0	3 2 1 0	3 2 1 0	3 2 1 0	3 2 1 0				
Big Little Pies	3 2 1 0	3 2 1 0	3 2 1 0	3 2 1 0	3 2 1 0	3 2 1 0	3 2 1 0				
Boardwalk Umpire	3 2 1 0	3 2 1 0	3 2 1 0	3 2 1 0	3 2 1 0	3 2 1 0	3 2 1 0				
Breaking Bald	3 2 1 0	3 2 1 0	3 2 1 0	3 2 1 0	3 2 1 0	3 2 1 0	3 2 1 0				
Counterparty	3 2 1 0	3 2 1 0	3 2 1 0	3 2 1 0	3 2 1 0	3 2 1 0	3 2 1 0				
Game of Clones	3 2 1 0	3 2 1 0	3 2 1 0	3 2 1 0	3 2 1 0	3 2 1 0	3 2 1 0				
Masters of Hex	3 2 1 0	3 2 1 0	3 2 1 0	3 2 1 0	3 2 1 0	3 2 1 0	3 2 1 0				
Outlandish	3 2 1 0	3 2 1 0	3 2 1 0	3 2 1 0	3 2 1 0	3 2 1 0	3 2 1 0				
Truly Bloody	3 2 1 0	3 2 1 0	3 2 1 0	3 2 1 0	3 2 1 0	3 2 1 0	3 2 1 0				
Twin Beaks	3 2 1 0	3 2 1 0	3 2 1 0	3 2 1 0	3 2 1 0	3 2 1 0	3 2 1 0				
Points											

Murder in the Guest Wing

The seven guests and Nolan are assuming the roles of high-stakes poker players. After an afternoon session of Texas hold'em that took place in the small game room, the guests went to various other locations in or around the mansion. When Nolan failed to show up for dinner, the grounds were searched, and his body was found in the tunnel at the bottom of the secret passage in the crawlspace located in the guest wing. From the statements of the staff and guests, can you determine who the killer was? (After playing dead briefly, Nolan left with Cheryl to sail around the island.)

Statements by the Montagues:

1. Gordon: Since the basement door to the tunnel was locked, the only way to access the place where the body was found was through a closet in guest room 1B, 1C, 2B, or 2C. Since no one moved a body through any guest wing hall, the crime was committed in the killer's room. There is only one guilty party, who is the only guest whose statement may be false.

2. Nina: Cheryl is staying in a special guest room on the third floor and is not a suspect. Nolan was staying in the cottage but took part in the poker game along with all the other guests. The other guests—Aria, Brianna, Danny, Kelly, Steven, and Taylor—are each staying in a different one of the six guest rooms in the guest wing. They are acting the parts of poker players whose main occupations are, in some combination, haberdasher, illusionist, judge, locksmith, marketer, and neurologist.

Statements by the staff:

3. Alistair: Nolan believed that one of the players had cheated at hold'em by introducing a marked deck of cards into the game, and he intended to search that person's room for evidence.

4. Charlotte: While conducting his search, Nolan was discovered by the killer, who stabbed him to death and pushed his body into the crawlspace connected to the closet in the same room. The body fell to the tunnel that leads to the basement.

5. Evelyn: The judge, the marketer, and the neurologist occupy rooms 1C, 2A, and 2B, in some combination, but the marketer is not in 2A.

6. Grant: The illusionist, the locksmith, and Taylor have rooms with three different letters.

7. Lyle: The illusionist and neurologist are in rooms with different letters.

8. Sandy: The occupant of room 1C is innocent, as are the illusionist and marketer.

Statements by the guests:

9. Aria: The other five guests' statements are true.

10. Brianna: The judge's room and mine have different letters.

11. Danny: Steven, Taylor, and I occupy rooms on the first floor.

12. Kelly: Brianna, Steven, and Taylor are the haberdasher, illusionist, and locksmith, in some combination.

13. Steven: The judge's room and mine have different letters.

14. Taylor: Kelly's room and mine have different letters.

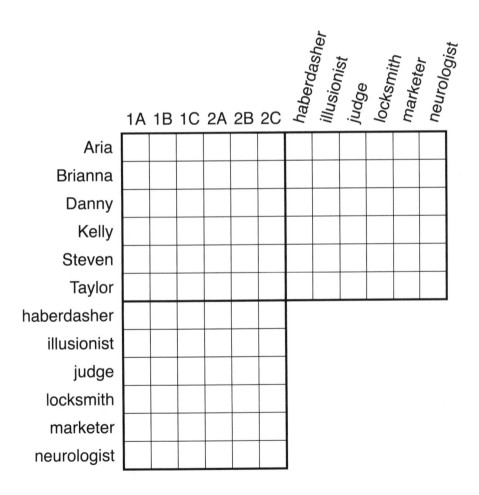

1830

Cheryl has convinced the other guests (Aria, Brianna, Danny, Kelly, Steven, and Taylor) as well as Nolan to take part in a two-day 18xx tournament. 18xx is the general name for more than 100 different board games based on stock trading and railroad development (some of which can now be played online with the Java program Rails). The object is to have the most money when the game ends, which happens when any player goes bankrupt or the bank runs out of money. Apart from the chance determination of the order of play on the first turn, which confers no discernible advantage to anyone, the game has no hidden information or random moves. Players begin with equal amounts of money.

The game chosen for the first day is 1830, which is set mostly in the northeastern United States. It was originally published by Avalon Hill in 1986. Because the game works best with four players, lots are drawn to divide the players into two groups of four. The small game room has only one copy of the game, and so one group will play in the morning and the other in the afternoon. (Games of 1830 typically last four or five hours.) The plan is for the top two finishers in each game, based on final cash totals, to meet the next day and play a different 18xx game to determine the winner of the tournament.

After a phase in which six small private companies are auctioned off, players with enough money may start up any of eight public railroad companies: Baltimore & Ohio (B&O); Boston & Maine (B&M); Canadian Pacific (CPR); Chesapeake & Ohio (C&O); Erie (Erie); New York Central (NYC); New York, New Haven & Hartford (NYNH); and Pennsylvania (PRR). The owners (majority stockholders) in a company operate it by buying trains, laying track, and running trains between cities to earn money. Majority ownership of a public company can change during a game, as shares in companies continue to be bought and sold, but in this puzzle the player who starts up a railroad owns it throughout the game.

From the clues below, can you determine who played in which game, which player owned each public company in each game, and the order in which the players in each game finished?

1. In both games, each player owned two public companies.

2. In the morning game, Taylor did better than the owner of the PRR, who did better than Aria.

3. In one game, the PRR owner finished ahead of Kelly, who finished ahead of the owner of the NYC.

4. In one game, the owner of the Erie did better than Danny, who finished ahead of the owner of the CPR.

5. In one game, Cheryl did better than the owner of the B&O, who did better than Steven.

6. Playing in different games, Nolan finished two places better than Brianna.

7. The PRR owner finished third in the game that Nolan played.

8. One of the public companies was owned by Steven and Taylor in different games.

9. In both games, the same player owned both the B&M and PRR.

10. The owners of the C&O finished fourth in both games.

11. The owners of the B&O finished in the same place in both games.

12. The owners of the NYNH finished first and second in the two games.

13. Neither owner of the NYC came in fourth.

14. Neither owner of the Erie came in first.

15. Taylor did not own the NYC.

16. Brianna did not own the B&M.

| | Morning | | | | Afternoon | | | | B&M | B&O | C&O | CPR | Erie | NYC | NYNH | PRR |
	1st	2nd	3rd	4th	1st	2nd	3rd	4th								
Aria																
Brianna																
Cheryl																
Danny																
Kelly																
Nolan																
Steven																
Taylor																
B&M									
B&O									
C&O									
CPR									
Erie									
NYC									
NYNH									
PRR									

1856

As planned, the top two finishers in each of the previous day's preliminary games met in a four-player final. This time the game used was 1856, published by Mayfair Games in the 1990s. The game is set in Upper Canada, the predecessor of modern-day Ontario.

Like 1830, 1856 is a game of stock trading and railway development in which the object is to have the most money when the game ends, which happens when any player goes bankrupt or the bank runs out of money. Players begin with equal amounts of money.

To begin the game, six private companies are auctioned off to the players. From least to most expensive in terms of the minimum required opening bid, these are: Flos Tramway, Waterloo & Saugeen Railway Co., the Canada Company, Great Lakes Shipping Company, Niagara Falls Suspension Bridge Company, and St. Clair Frontier Tunnel Company. (These provide some revenue to their owners and can confer certain advantages in play.) After that, players with enough money may start up any of 11 public railway companies: Buffalo, Brantford & Goderich (BBG); Canada Air Line (CA); Canadian Pacific (CPR); Credit Valley (CV); Grand Trunk (GT); Great Western (GW); London & Port Sarnia (LPS); Toronto, Grey & Bruce (TGB); Toronto, Hamilton & Buffalo (THB); Welland (WR); and Wellington, Grey & Bruce (WGB). Majority ownership of a public company can change during a game as stocks are bought and sold; but in this puzzle, each player who starts a company owns and operates it throughout the game. (The Canadian Government Railways sometimes becomes a 12th company, absorbing companies that are at risk of bankruptcy, but that did not happen in this particular game.)

Between stock rounds, players operate railroads to earn money, giving the company's majority owners a dilemma: whether to use the money to pay dividends to company shareholders, raising the company's stock value, or to keep the money in the company, lowering the stock value but facilitating future train purchases, which must be made as older trains become obsolete.

From the clues below, can you determine which player bought which private company or companies at auction, which player owned each public company, and the order in which the players finished?

1. The player who finished third, the player who bought the Great Lakes Shipping Company, and Cheryl each owned three different public companies, none of which was CA or CPR.

2. The player who finished first, the player who bought the Canada Company, and Kelly together owned all the public companies except BBG, THB, and WR.

3. Taylor and the buyer of Flos Tramway owned CV and GW, not necessarily in that order.

4. The buyer of the Canada Company owned LPS and WGB.

5. The buyers of the Niagara Falls Suspension Bridge Company and St. Clair Frontier Tunnel Company finished third and fourth, not necessarily in that order.

6. The owner of GT, who bought at least one of the six private companies, finished ahead of the owner of GW.

7. The owner of WGB finished ahead of the owner of THB.

8. Cheryl finished one place better than the buyer of the Niagara Falls Suspension Bridge Company.

9. One player bought both the Waterloo & Saugeen Railway Co. and Great Lakes Shipping Company.

Major Arcana

Gordon is a fan of some old card games that use a 78-card tarot deck. As the basis for a puzzle, Gordon takes a portion of the deck—the major arcana, which comprise 22 cards numbered from 0 to 21 (for details, see the box on the next page)—and after removing the Fool (the card with value 0), shuffles and deals the cards out to the seven guests.

For the purposes of the puzzle, Gordon has classified the cards into four groups, based on their numbers: primes (numbers not a multiple of any number other than 1 and themselves); prime products (numbers that are a product of two different primes); squares (numbers that are the product of a number and itself); and leftovers (numbers fitting none of the other categories). The category for each number from 1 through 21 is shown in the grid.

From the following clues, can you determine each guest's three-card hand?

1. Cheryl, Kelly, and Steven each has a hand consisting of a prime, a prime product, and a square.

2. Aria and Danny each have a hand consisting of a prime, a prime product, and a leftover.

3. Taylor has a hand consisting of three primes.

4. The sum of the numbers on the cards in Brianna's hand is 1 less than in Steven's hand, 2 less than in Danny's hand, 3 less than in Aria's hand, and 4 less than in Cheryl's hand.

5. Steven has one of the three highest-numbered cards and at least one of the three lowest-numbered cards, and his only card with an even number is not a square.

6. Kelly's prime, which is not 17, is one less than the sum of Kelly's other two cards.

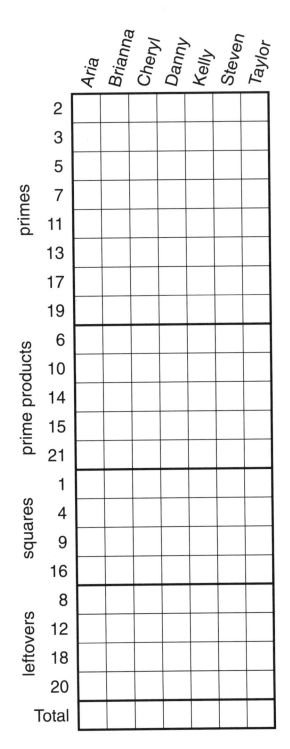

Tarot Decks

A typical 78-card tarot deck consists of four suits—often swords, batons (or wands), coins (or pentacles or disks), and cups. Each suit consists of 14 cards: ace through 10, jack (or knave), knight, queen, and king. The 22 major arcana are a kind of trump suit, with numbers and names as follows:

0 The Fool	7 The Chariot	15 The Devil
1 The Magician	8 Strength (or Justice)	16 The Tower
2 The High Priestess	9 The Hermit	17 The Star
3 The Empress	10 Wheel of Fortune	18 The Moon
4 The Emperor	11 Justice (or Strength)	19 The Sun
5 The Hierophant	12 The Hanged Man	20 Judgment
6 The Lovers	13 Death	21 The World
	14 Temperance	

Birdhouses

"We have six birdhouses scattered around the island, suitable for a variety of species," Gordon Montague explains to his guests. "If you'd like to check them out, you'll find one at or near six of the following locations: the boathouse, the bridge, the cottage, Duck Island, the lighthouse, Lookout Point, the mansion, the old hut, the old well, the pond, and the windmill.

"I couldn't resist making a little puzzle to help you find the birdhouses more easily. On this piece of paper I'm passing out, there are two sets of three statements each. Within each set, two statements are true and the other one is false. In each set, the false statement may be the first, second, or third statement. By using some logic, can you determine the six locations where you can find a birdhouse?"

Set #1

1. There are birdhouses near the boathouse and on Duck Island, but not near the old well.

2. There are birdhouses near the cottage and windmill, but not near Lookout Point.

3. There are birdhouses near the lighthouse and the pond, but not near the bridge.

Set #2

4. There are birdhouses near the bridge and the pond, but not near the boathouse.

5. There are birdhouses near the boathouse and the windmill, but not near the cottage.

6. There are birdhouses near the lighthouse and the mansion, but not near the old hut.

Wildflowers

On Friday night Gordon and Nina give all seven guests copies of a map of the island and a list of 20 different wildflowers (acony bell, atamasco lily, bloodroot, Canada violet, cardinal flower, Carolina jasmine, common toadflax, coral honeysuckle, crane-fly orchid, fire pink, heliotrope, jack-in-the-pulpit, little sweet Betsy, mayapple, prickly-pear cactus, spiderwort, trailing bluet, trillium, windflower, and yellow passionflower) that the Montagues have previously planted at a total of 10 different locations on the island (boathouse, bridge, cottage, Duck Island, lighthouse, Lookout Point, pond, old hut, old well, and windmill). The guests will look for these wildflowers between 9 A.M. and noon on Saturday, returning with a sample of each wildflower found. The guests are also furnished an illustrated book that will help them identify all the plants on the list. From the clues below, can you determine which wildflowers were brought back by each guest and the location where each kind of wildflower was found?

1. Three locations have one kind of wildflower, four locations have two kinds, and three locations have three kinds. No wildflower is found at more than one location.

2. Each guest visited exactly five locations and successfully found every wildflower at each place they visited, but no two guests came back with the same number of wildflower varieties.

3. One location was visited by just two guests, two locations were visited by all but two guests, and the other locations were visited by either three or four guests.

4. The total number of guests who visited locations with a single kind of wildflower was the same as the total number of guests who visited locations with three kinds of wildflowers.

5. Everyone except Cheryl and Taylor brought back yellow passionflower from the bridge.

6. Everyone except Brianna and Kelly brought back spiderwort from the old well.

7. Atamasco lily, mayapple, and trailing bluet were the only wildflowers brought back from Duck Island, the lighthouse, and the windmill, not necessarily in that order, none of which was a location visited by Danny.

8. The three guests who found heliotrope at the pond were Aria, a guest who found crane-fly orchid from Lookout Point, and a guest who found windflower at the boathouse.

9. Two of the three guests who found little sweet Betsy and fire pink at the cottage were Danny and Kelly.

10. Everyone who went to the old hut went to the old well; and except for Danny and Taylor, everyone who went to the old well also went to the old hut.

11. The three who went to the windmill were Cheryl, Steven, and one who brought back a Canada violet—which was also brought back by either Cheryl or Steven but not both.

12. Danny, who did not visit the boathouse, had only one location in common with Brianna.

13. Only one location was visited by both Aria and Brianna, but Brianna and Kelly visited four of the same locations.

14. More wildflower varieties could be found at the cottage, Lookout Point, or the pond than at the boathouse, which was visited by four guests.

15. Mayapple and prickly-pear cactus were found at the only two locations visited by both Brianna and Cheryl.

16. Steven, who did not visit the lighthouse, brought back trailing bluet.

17. At one location Cheryl, Danny, and Taylor all found Carolina jasmine and common toadflax.
18. Jack-in-the-pulpit and trillium were not the only wildflower varieties at their location.
19. Bloodroot and coral honeysuckle were at the same location.
20. One of the 11 wildflower varieties collected by one guest was cardinal flower.

Columns: boathouse, bridge, cottage, Duck Island, lighthouse, Lookout Point, pond, old hut, old well, windmill, Aria, Brianna, Cheryl, Danny, Kelly, Steven, Taylor

Rows:
- acony bell
- atamasco lily
- bloodroot
- Canada violet
- cardinal flower
- Carolina jasmine
- common toadflax
- coral honeysuckle
- crane-fly orchid
- fire pink
- heliotrope
- jack-in-the-pulpit
- little sweet Betsy
- mayapple
- prickly-pear cactus
- spiderwort
- trailing bluet
- trillium
- windflower
- yellow passionflower
- Aria
- Brianna
- Cheryl
- Danny
- Kelly
- Steven
- Taylor
- kinds of wildflowers
- number of guests

wildflowers found

37

Murder at the Lighthouse

The guests are playing people of various occupations, who are all directors of a botanical garden. The group is meeting this weekend at the home of the Montagues, who are also members of the board. On Saturday, the board met from 10 A.M. until noon. Another meeting was planned for 2:30, but it was canceled when a murder victim, played by Nolan, was discovered around 2:00. From the statements of the Montagues, their staff, and the guests, can you determine the occupation of each guest, where each guest was during each half-hour period between 12 noon and 1:30 P.M., and the identity of the killer?

Statements by the Montagues:

1. Gordon: After our morning meeting in the lounge ended, Nina and I took walk to the pond. Later we learned that a contractor we had asked to give an estimate on painting the lighthouse came by around 12:15 to speak to us, then asked us to meet him at the lighthouse later. We got there a little before 2 P.M. and discovered that the contractor had been murdered.

2. Nina: The victim was fatally pushed from the top of the lighthouse's spiral staircase. We found a note the victim had written for us, which the killer didn't notice, saying that he recognized one of our guests as a wanted fugitive who had embezzled a large sum from a company where the guest and victim both used to work in Seattle.

Statements by the staff:

3. Alistair: The occupations of the seven board members other than the Montagues are oceanographer, promoter, quizmaster, rancher, speculator, teacher, and undertaker. When the victim was here, any of the guests might have overheard him tell me to ask the Montagues to meet him at the lighthouse.

4. Charlotte: All guests were in the mansion before 12 noon and after 1:30 P.M. Between noon and 1:30, each guest who was in the mansion spent their time in the dining room, the lounge, and/or the small game room. Guests did not change rooms except at 12:30 and/or 1. In one of the half-hour time periods, three guests occupied the lounge.

5. Evelyn: Each guest spent at least half an hour in the dining room. Danny spent just one half-hour period there, during the period before the undertaker was there.

6. Grant: Cheryl, who is not the quizmaster, was in the small game room for the first two half-hour periods. Three guests were in the small game room during two of the half-hour periods.

7. Lyle: All the guests' statements are true.

8. Sandy: It would have taken the killer more than half an hour to go from the mansion to the lighthouse and back.

Statements by the guests:

9. Aria: During one of the half-hour periods, the three people in the dining room were myself, the promoter, and the undertaker.

10. Brianna: During one of the half-hour periods, the three people in the dining room were myself, the oceanographer, and the rancher.

11. Cheryl: During each of the three half-hour periods, the teacher and I were in the same room.

12. Danny: During one of the half-hour time periods, the quizmaster and I were the only guests in the dining room.

13. Kelly: During each of the three half-hour periods, the promoter and I were in the same room.

14. Steven: I was in the small game room for two consecutive half-hour periods.

15. Taylor: The oceanographer and I were in different rooms from one another during each of the half-hour time periods. I was in all three rooms, and each time the same number of other guests were in the room with me.

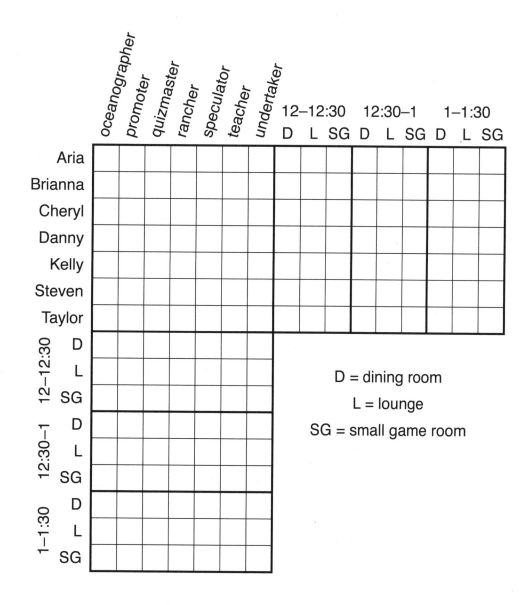

Amusement Park

"We're going to check out Thrill Island today, the amusement park that opened last year," Cheryl reminds Gordon and Nina at breakfast. "It might be a good place to take our friends when they visit in a couple of weeks. Do you want to come along?"

Gordon shakes his head. "No thanks—Nina and I are working on a project in the greenhouse. Maybe next time."

The seven guests proceed to the boathouse, where Nolan is waiting to take them to the mainland in the cabin cruiser. Thrill Island—which is actually on a peninsula—is a few miles up the coast from the usual place that the cabin cruiser docks, and so the trip took nearly an hour. A restaurant at the amusement park has its own pier where boats may conveniently dock as long as their occupants will be patronizing the restaurant or the amusement park.

"There's a security guard who keeps an eye on the pier, but just to be on the safe side, I think I'll stay on the boat," Nolan explains. "I'll see you all back here around 4:00."

The guests wasted no time trying out several of the park's many rides, then tried their luck on the carnival midway. It took some of the guests several attempts, but everyone eventually won a prize. From the clues below, can you determine each guest's favorite ride and who won what prize by playing which game?

1. Each guest had a different favorite ride among the following: bumper boats, carousel, drop tower, Ferris wheel, pirate ship, roller coaster, Tilt-A-Whirl.

2. Each guest won a prize by playing one of the following games: balloon and dart, basketball, coin toss, high striker, milk bottle, Skee-Ball, and water gun. No two guests won prizes at the same game.

3. The seven prizes won by the guests were the following plush animals: alligator, dog, lion, panda, tiger, whale, zebra.

4. The favorite rides of Brianna, Danny, and Taylor were the drop tower, Ferris wheel, and pirate ship, in some combination.

5. The alligator, panda, and zebra were won by playing balloon and dart, coin toss, and Skee-Ball, in some combination.

6. The guests whose favorite rides were the pirate ship, roller coaster, and Tilt-A-Whirl won prizes at balloon and dart, basketball, and high striker, in some combination.

7. Cheryl, Danny, and Steven won a dog, a lion, and a panda, in some combination.

8. The guests whose favorite rides were bumper boats, roller coaster, and Tilt-A-Whirl won a lion, a panda, and a tiger, in some combination.

9. Kelly, Steven, and Taylor won prizes at basketball, milk bottle, and water gun, in some combination.

10. Of the two guests who, between them, won the alligator and won a prize from Skee-Ball, neither chose the Ferris wheel as their favorite ride.

11. Of the two guests who, between them, chose bumper boats as their favorite ride and won a prize by playing water gun, neither won a tiger.

12. The guest whose favorite ride was the Tilt-A-Whirl did not win a panda, and the guest whose favorite ride was the carousel did not win a zebra.

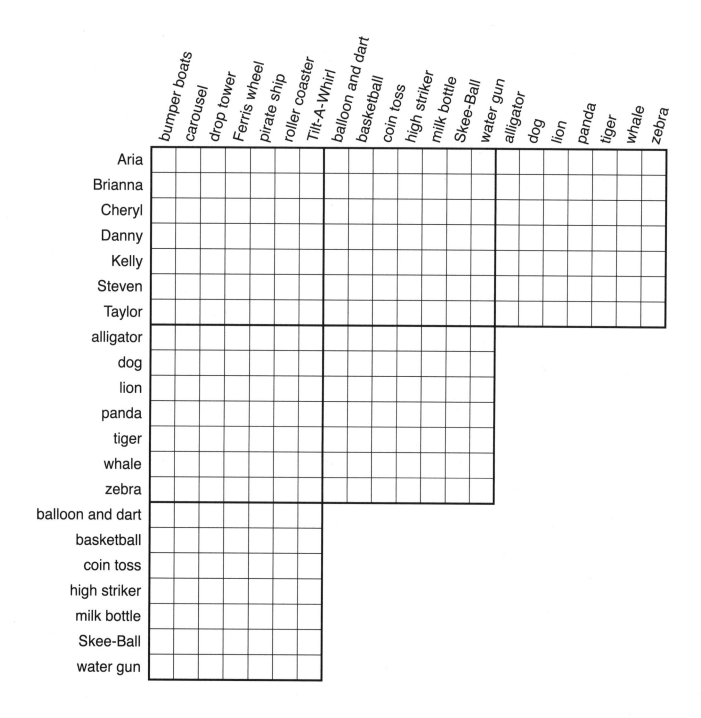

Miniature Golf

Around 3 P.M., Cheryl judges there is still time to try out the amusement park's miniature golf course. She persuades Aria, Brianna, and Danny to join her to make a foursome.

The 18-hole course had three different themes. The first six holes, viewed from above, are shaped like different letters of the alphabet. The middle six holes incorporate various man-made structures. The final six holes involve natural physical features.

Aria, Brianna, Cheryl, and Danny played all 18 holes. From the clues below, can you determine how they scored on each hole and their order of finish? As in regular golf, the player with the lowest score (fewest strokes taken) wins.

1. On every hole, each player scored either a birdie (one under par), a par, or a bogey (one over par).

2. Aria scored 3 on eight consecutive holes, and Danny had the next most consecutive 3's, with four.

3. Brianna had five consecutive birdies and Aria had the next most consecutive birdies, with four.

4. Cheryl had six consecutive bogeys, and Brianna had the next most consecutive bogeys, with four.

5. Danny had 10 consecutive pars.

6. Three different players had the best scores on the three sets of holes with common themes (1–6, 7–12, and 13–18), but none of these players had the lowest total score.

7. Two players had identical scores on each of the first four holes, and the other two players had identical scores on each of the holes 4 through 9.

8. The players recorded three different scores on hole 14 as well as on hole 17, and Danny had the same score on holes 1 and 14.

9. Altogether the players had eight 1's (holes-in-one), of which Brianna had the most and Danny the fewest.

10. The players' scores matched each other on hole 8. The players' scores also matched each other on hole 18.

11. On no hole did the sum of the players' four scores add up to the hole number.

12. Only Cheryl had a hole-in-one on the front nine (holes 1–9), and everyone but Cheryl had a hole-in-one on the 13th hole.

13. The same three players had 2's on holes 2 and 3, which were all of the 2's on those holes.

14. All four players scored the same on the 16th hole as they had on the 2nd.

15. Brianna had more 2's than Cheryl did.

16. Brianna did not have a hole-in-one on the 10th hole.

	Par	Aria	Brianna	Cheryl	Danny
1. The L	2				
2. The T	2				
3. The U	3				
4. The Y	2				
5. The Z	3				
6. The W	4				
First Third Total	16				
7. The Tunnel	2				
8. The Bridge	3				
9. The Castle	3				
10. The Ramp	2				
11. The Loop	3				
12. The Windmill	3				
Middle Third Total	16				
13. The Cave	2				
14. The Plateau	2				
15. The Cliffs	4				
16. The Waterfall	2				
17. The Lake	2				
18. The Hills	4				
Final Third Total	16				
Total Score	48				

Hard Candy

Before leaving Thrill Island, the guests stop at three small candy shops near the pier—Guilty Pleasures, Olde Candy Shoppe, and Sweet Dreams—where each guest buys a different flavor of hard candy: apple, butterscotch, cinnamon, orange, peppermint, raspberry, and strawberry. Each guest soon shares part of his or her candy with one other guest. From the clues below, can you determine who bought which flavors, the shop where each candy was purchased, and the guest with whom each guest shared his or her candy?

1. Aria, Cheryl, and Taylor bought cinnamon, peppermint, and strawberry hard candy, in some combination.

2. The apple, cinnamon, and strawberry hard candy was shared with Aria, Kelly, and Steven, in some combination.

3. The two guests who bought candy at Guilty Pleasures shared it with Aria and Danny.

4. Candy bought at the Olde Candy Shoppe was shared with Steven and Taylor.

5. One of the guests who bought candy at Sweet Dreams shared it with Kelly.

6. Candy bought at a particular store was never shared with a guest who bought candy at that store.

7. The butterscotch candy and cinnamon candy were bought at the same store.

8. The raspberry candy and strawberry candy were bought at the same store.

9. In one shop, the only two people who bought candy were Cheryl and Steven.

10. Danny bought candy at the same store where other guests bought orange candy and peppermint candy.

11. Brianna, Danny, and Steven shared candy with one another, in some combination.

12. Aria shared candy with Cheryl.

13. The butterscotch candy was shared with Danny.

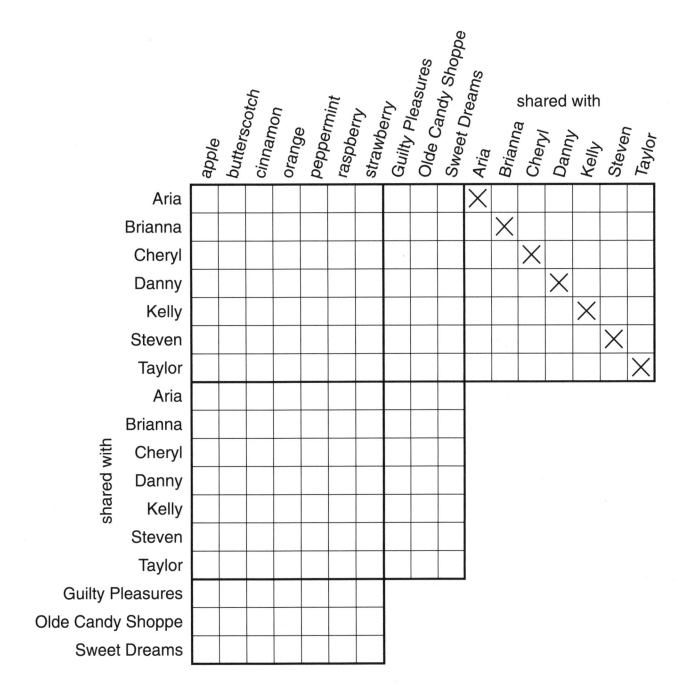

Fantasy Chess Draft

Fantasy sports leagues typically begin by holding a draft in which participants take turns selecting desired players at costs reflecting each player's perceived value. Gordon Montague is experimenting with a new kind of fantasy draft, one in which players select what movement powers their chess pieces will have. After the draft, the six participating players will play a round-robin tournament using their own customized chess armies each game.

Players will all begin with a standard king and eight pawns, but must draft seven more pieces to complete their armies. Players are required to select three pairs of identical pieces and one unpaired piece, making it easier to use standard chess sets to represent the new pieces.

Each player has 19 points to spend on drafting pieces, which is what a standard chess army would cost under Gordon's rules. Nineteen different types of pieces are available: six "basic" pieces with a single type of movement power, and 13 "combo" pieces that combine the movement powers of two different basic pieces. The point cost for each piece and the quantity of each piece available to be drafted are shown in a table on the next page. Note that each combo piece's cost is equal to the sum of the costs of its component basic pieces.

The basic pieces are represented by the symbols R, B, N, C, F, and W, each of which represents a specific movement power. R (rook) pieces move in any unobstructed horizontal or vertical direction, B (bishop) pieces move in any unobstructed diagonal direction, N (knight) pieces leap from one corner to the opposite one of any 2×3 (or 3×2) rectangle of squares, C (camel) pieces leap from one corner to the opposite one of any 2×4 (or 4×2) rectangle of squares, F (ferz) pieces move one square in any diagonal direction, and W (wazir) pieces move one square in any horizontal or vertical direction. (The ferz and wazir appear in certain historical chess variants.)

A combo piece has the ability to move as either of its two lettered movements. For example, an R+B piece can move as either a rook or a bishop on a given turn (like a queen in chess). B+W could move diagonally as a bishop or move a single square horizontally or vertically (like a dragon horse in shogi). N+C could jump as either a knight or a camel (like a wildebeest in Wildebeest Chess). The combinations B+F and R+W are not used, since B movement includes F movement and R movement includes W movement.

The order in which players draft pieces for the first round is determined randomly. During each round a player may either draft a single piece or a pair of identical pieces. After four rounds, the player must have drafted three pairs and one single piece without spending more than 19 points.

Gordon advises players that in the simplified point cost scale used in the draft, certain pieces are somewhat overpriced (most notably the camel) and others are underpriced (such as the ferz). Most pieces that combine two moves are underpriced, as they are usually worth more than the sum of their component moves. In chess, for example, it is well established that a queen is worth about a pawn more than a rook and a bishop.

The six players proceed to draft their armies. From the following clues, can you determine who drafted which pieces in which rounds? Note: When a clue refers to a piece by letter, the piece may be a basic piece with the lettered power or any combo piece including that letter. For example, a "B piece" means either a B, R+B, B+N, B+C, or B+W piece.

1. The draft order in each of the four rounds was: Aria, Cheryl, Danny, Gordon, Steven, Taylor.

2. Each player used up all 19 available points in drafting three pairs of pieces and a single piece. Pieces drafted by a player in different rounds could not be of the same type, although they could share one movement power.

3. Aria spent 8 points in each of the first two rounds, and Cheryl spent 8 points in the second round.

4. Two players in succession drafted single pieces in the first round, and all the other players drafted their single pieces in the fourth round.

5. Only four C pieces were drafted, in two pairs, and exactly eight other drafts happened between them.

6. The first seven pieces drafted in the first round were B pieces, and the last six pieces drafted in the first round were R pieces.

7. Exactly half the pieces that were drafted were basic pieces.

8. Every player drafted a different number of combo pieces, with Taylor drafting the fewest.

9. Gordon drafted four N pieces and four W pieces.

10. No W pieces were drafted in the second round.

11. All the basic B and F pieces (four of each) were drafted.

12. A pair of basic R pieces was drafted immediately before a pair of basic B pieces.

13. Two pairs of basic N pieces were drafted in different rounds.

14. Cheryl's pieces collectively had five different types of movement, as did Steven's pieces.

15. In the final round, two people each drafted a pair of the same kind of basic piece, and two people drafted the same kind of single basic piece.

	Aria	Cheryl	Danny	Gordon	Steven	Taylor
Round 1						
Round 2						
Round 3						
Round 4						

Piece	Pts	Qty
R	3	4
B	2	4
N	2	4
C	2	4
F	1	4
W	1	12
R+B	5	3
R+N	5	3
R+C	5	3
R+F	4	3
B+N	4	3
B+C	4	3
N+C	4	3
B+W	3	2
N+F	3	2
C+F	3	2
N+W	3	2
C+W	3	2
F+W	2	2

Fantasy Chess Tournament

After the fantasy chess army draft, Gordon applied a more sophisticated evaluation of the pieces than their draft costs and ranked the six armies from strongest (rank of 1) to weakest (6). (Details about Gordon's ranking system are provided in the answer to this puzzle.) He then worked out a schedule in which each of the six players (Aria, Cheryl, Danny, Gordon, Steven, and Taylor) would play the other once, with three games being played simultaneously in each of five rounds. The choice of color in each game was not arbitrary: Whichever player's army was ranked weaker moved first (played White) each game, and the stronger army always played Black. During the games, players could refer to note cards reminding them of the movement powers of all the pieces in the game.

From the clues below, can you determine who played whom each round, what each player's result was each round (win, loss, or draw), how each player's army ranked in strength, and what each player's total score in the tournament was? A player earns 1 point for each win, half a point for each draw, and nothing for a loss. The player with the most points wins the tournament.

1. The only undefeated player did not finish first.

2. The strongest army met the second-strongest army in round 5 and the weakest army in round 1.

3. Adding 1 to the army rank of three of the players yields their point total.

4. The players with the four highest point totals each had half a point more than the player who finished just below them.

5. In round 1 Cheryl and Taylor, both playing White, defeated Danny and Aria, respectively.

6. Cheryl lost to Aria in round 4 and played Steven in round 5.

7. In rounds 3 and 4, Gordon had draws with two players who drew against one another in round 5.

8. Gordon played White more times than Taylor but fewer times than Steven.

	Round 1 vs. ?	Round 2 vs. ?	Round 3 vs. ?	Round 4 vs. ?	Round 5 vs. ?	Army rank	Won	Lost	Drawn	Total points
Aria	W L D	W L D	W L D	W L D	W L D					
Cheryl	W L D	W L D	W L D	W L D	W L D					
Danny	W L D	W L D	W L D	W L D	W L D					
Gordon	W L D	W L D	W L D	W L D	W L D					
Steven	W L D	W L D	W L D	W L D	W L D					
Taylor	W L D	W L D	W L D	W L D	W L D					

Seven, Zero

Taylor explains the rules of a logic-oriented word game to the guests. It's a variation on the classic deduction game of bulls and cows, or the trademarked games Mastermind and Jotto. Taylor will think of a secret word, which must be a reasonably common, uncapitalized seven-letter word composed of seven different letters of the alphabet. (The last time Taylor played this game on Montague Island, six-letter words were used.) The other players take turns guessing the word aloud, and after each guess (which must also be a reasonably common seven-letter word composed of all different letters) Taylor states a pair of numbers. The first number indicates the number of letters in the guess that match letters in the secret word and are in the same position within the word, and the second number indicates how many letters in the guess are in the secret word but are not in the same position.

For example, if the secret word were DESTINY and the guess were RETAINS, Taylor would say "three, two" since three matching letters (E, I, N) are in the same position in both words, and two other letters (S, T) are also in both words but in different positions.

The first three guesses and Taylor's replies are:

Aria:	VICTORY	1,2
Brianna:	CLOSING	1,2
Cheryl:	INSTEAD	0,5
Danny:	TACKLED	1,5

At this point Kelly says, "I know what the secret word is!"

Then Steven says, "I know it, too, and it has a common anagram that can be found by giving different answers to the same four guess words." He writes down the following alternative answers to the guess words:

VICTORY	1,2
CLOSING	0,3
INSTEAD	1,4
TACKLED	0,6

Can you determine the word Kelly found and the anagram pointed out by Steven?

Taylor suggests a bonus puzzle: Can you find an uncommon anagram of the word that also fits Steven's alternative answers?

Around Midnight

The guests are playing wealthy individuals who both collect and occasionally sell expensive paintings. Recently each guest has bought a painting from another guest and sold a different painting to a different other guest. After the sales, one of the guests discovered that the painting he or she had purchased was a forgery, and tried to force the seller to undo the transaction. When confronted shortly after midnight, however, the seller covered up the fraudulent sale by silencing the buyer permanently.

From the clues below, can you determine who bought which paintings from whom, what buyers were alone with their sellers after midnight, and discover who murdered whom?

1. Each guest bought one of the following paintings from another guest: *American Goths, Christina's Whirl, Garden of Early Delights, Persistence of Melody, The Screamer, Starry Knight*, and *Whistler's Grandma*. No one bought a painting from the person to whom he or she sold a painting.

2. Just before midnight, each guest was in one of four locations: art studio, game alcove, guest wing, screened porch. At midnight, five guests moved to a different one of these locations, and two stayed where they were. No more than two guests were in a single location either before midnight or after midnight.

3. Cheryl, Danny, and Kelly were the sellers of *Garden of Early Delights, Persistence of Melody*, and *The Screamer*, in some combination.

4. Aria, Cheryl, and Danny were the buyers of *American Goths, Christina's Whirl*, and *Whistler's Grandma*, in some combination.

5. Neither Steven nor Taylor was the buyer or seller of *Starry Knight*.

6. One guest bought *American Goths* and sold *Whistler's Grandma*.

7. The buyer of *Starry Knight* and the seller of *Garden of Early Delights* were together in the art studio before midnight.

8. The buyer of *American Goths* and the seller of *Christina's Whirl* were together in the art studio after midnight.

9. The buyer of *Persistence of Melody* and the seller of *Starry Knight* were together in the game alcove before midnight.

10. The seller of *Persistence of Melody* was in the game alcove after midnight.

11. The buyer of *The Screamer* and the seller of *Whistler's Grandma* were together in the guest wing before midnight.

12. The seller of *The Screamer* was on the screened porch before midnight.

13. The buyer of *Christina's Whirl* was in the guest wing after midnight.

14. The seller of *The Screamer* bought *Whistler's Grandma*.

15. At midnight Danny went from the art studio to the guest wing.

16. Steven was in both the art studio and game alcove, not necessarily in that order.

17. Taylor, who was on the screened porch either before or after midnight, never sold or purchased a forged painting and so was not a murderer or murder victim.

	painting's seller							painting's buyer						
	Aria	Brianna	Cheryl	Danny	Kelly	Steven	Taylor	Aria	Brianna	Cheryl	Danny	Kelly	Steven	Taylor
American Goths														
Christina's Whirl														
Garden of Early Delights														
Persistence of Melody														
The Screamer														
Starry Knight														
Whistler's Grandma														
Aria	✕													
Brianna		✕												
Cheryl			✕											
Danny				✕										
Kelly					✕									
Steven						✕								
Taylor							✕							

(left label: painting's buyer)

	Art Studio		Game Alcove		Guest Wing		Screened Porch	
	before 12	after 12	before 12	after 12	before 12	after 12	before 12	after 12
Aria								
Brianna								
Cheryl								
Danny								
Kelly								
Steven								
Taylor								

Who's Whose

In celebration of having taken their bar exams, five of the guests (Aria, Brianna, Danny, Kelly, Steven) have each invited a recent acquaintance to the island for the weekend. Cheryl plans to spend her time with Nolan, talking about what her new job means for their future.

The invitees have furnished Cheryl with certain information about themselves as the basis for her making a puzzle. From the clues that follow, can you determine who invited whom, the occupations of the invitees, the place where each guest and invitee first met, and what each invitee named as his or her all-time favorite TV series?

1. The invitees—Hugh, John, Morgan, Rachel, Wendy—work, not necessarily respectively, as a bartender, graphic artist, systems analyst, x-ray technician, and video editor. The places where the guests and invitees first met, again not necessarily respectively, were a 5K race, an art museum, a nature center, a political rally, and a volleyball game. The invitees' all-time favorite TV series, again not respectively, are *The Americans*, *Buffy the Vampire Slayer*, *Friday Night Lights*, *The 100*, and *The Wire*.

2. The bartender and the video editor first met the guests who invited them at a political rally and a volleyball game, in some combination.

3. Brianna and Kelly invited the two whose favorite series are *The Americans* and *The Wire*, in some combination.

4. *Friday Night Lights* and *The 100* are the favorite series of Morgan and Rachel, in some combination.

5. The favorite series of the graphic artist and x-ray technician are *Friday Night Lights* and *The Wire*, in some combination.

6. John and Wendy are the graphic artist and video editor, in some combination.

7. Danny and Steven first met their invitees at a nature center and a volleyball game, in some order.

8. Aria and Kelly invited the graphic artist and systems analyst, in some combination.

9. Aria did not meet her invitee at an art museum.

10. The favorite series of the video editor, who was not invited by Steven, was not *The Americans*.

11. John's favorite series is not *Buffy the Vampire Slayer*, and Morgan has never been to a 5K race.

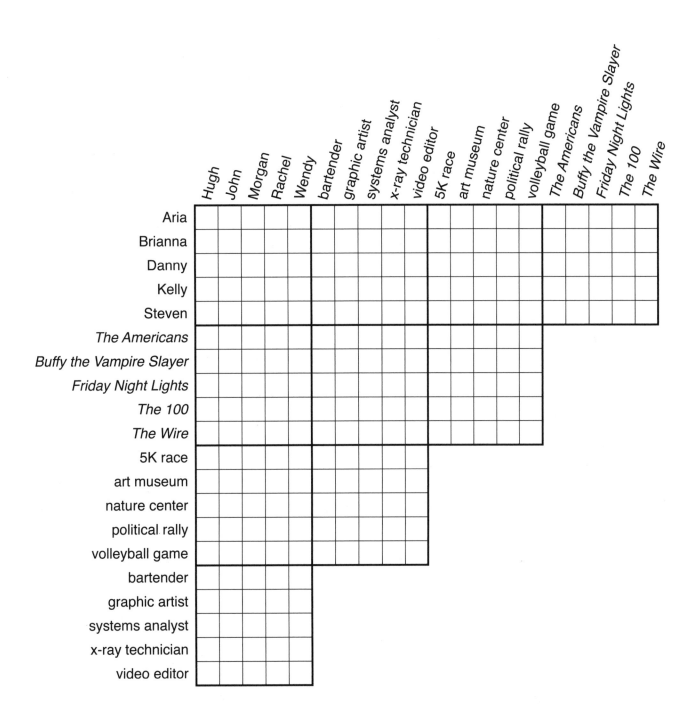

Thrill Island Excursion

Nolan is piloting the Montagues' cabin cruiser to Thrill Island, the amusement park visited by the guests earlier in the summer. Aboard are the Montagues, their seven guests, and the five friends that some of those guests have invited to the island for the weekend. After tying the boat at the pier that serves a restaurant as well as the park, Nolan says a few words to the security guard who watches the pier before joining the others as they enter the park.

Over the next few hours everyone takes a few rides and takes time to eat a couple of snacks. From the clues below, can you determine which ride was each person's favorite and what two snacks each person had from among the six kinds of foods that were eaten by the group?

1. Each person had a favorite ride that he or she took multiple times. In all, eight different rides were the favorites of at least one of the party of 15: Caterpillar, Gyro Tower, Log Flume, Loop-the-Loop, Octopus, Round Up, Teacups, and Tunnel of Love.

2. Each person consumed two of the following foods: churro, corn dog, cotton candy, fried cheese curds, funnel cake, and soft pretzel. No two people ate the same combination of two foods.

3. No two people who had the same favorite ride ate any of the same kinds of food.

4. The favorite rides of Aria, Brianna, Cheryl, Danny, and Gordon were, in some order, Caterpillar, Gyro Tower, Loop-the-Loop, Teacups, and Tunnel of Love.

5. The favorite rides of Hugh, Kelly, Nina, Rachel, and Taylor were, in some order, Caterpillar, Log Flume, Loop-the-Loop, Octopus, and Tunnel of Love.

6. The favorite rides of John, Morgan, Nolan, Steven, and Wendy were, in some order, Gyro Tower, Loop-the-Loop, Octopus, Round Up, and Teacups.

7. Aria and Steven had the same favorite ride, as did the following pairs: Brianna and Rachel, Danny and Morgan, and Gordon and Nina.

8. The person whose favorite ride was the Log Flume ate churro and fried cheese curds.

9. The person whose favorite ride was the Round Up ate cotton candy and funnel cake.

10. Aria, Cheryl, Hugh, Morgan, and Taylor all ate one of the same food items.

11. Cheryl, John, Nina, Rachel, and Wendy all ate one of the same food items.

12. Gordon, Kelly, Morgan, Steven, and Wendy all ate one of the same food items.

13. Nina's favorite ride was not the Loop-the-Loop.

14. Aria, Danny, and Rachel each had a soft pretzel.

15. John and Taylor ate fried cheese curds.

16. Gordon had funnel cake.

17. One of those favoring Teacups had fried cheese curds, which no one favoring the Tunnel of Love ate.

18. Nolan did not have a corn dog.

Paintball

After the amusement park, the guests and their visitors, as well as Nolan, decide to try a nearby paintball course, where Taylor and the Montagues are content to be spectators. The paintball players agree to a simple elimination game with two teams of six: the guests (Aria, Brianna, Cheryl, Danny, Kelly, and Steven) on one team and their visitors (Hugh, John, Morgan, Rachel, and Wendy) plus Nolan on the other team.

They don protective eyewear and ponchos to protect their clothing, choose paintball guns and paint colors, and proceed to the indoor course, where barriers are randomly set up to provide temporary cover as people try to shoot the other team's players without getting shot. When a player is hit by a ball of paint that leaves a mark, that player is tagged and is eliminated from the game.

From the clues below, can you determine who eliminated whom, and which team won by having the last surviving player?

1. Brianna was eliminated by Rachel, who was eliminated by Danny, who was eliminated by Morgan, who was eliminated by Kelly.

2. The number of players who were eliminated between the elimination of the following pairs of players were as follows: six players between Morgan and Steven, five players between Hugh and Rachel, four players between Cheryl and Wendy, four players between Brianna and Rachel, and three players between Aria and Brianna. The first player named in each pair was not necessarily eliminated before the other one.

3. Kelly, Morgan, and Nolan each eliminated two of the final seven people to be eliminated.

4. Cheryl, Danny, Morgan, and Nolan eliminated Aria, Hugh, Steven, and Wendy, in some combination.

5. One person was eliminated between the two people that Morgan eliminated.

6. Danny eliminated someone before Rachel did.

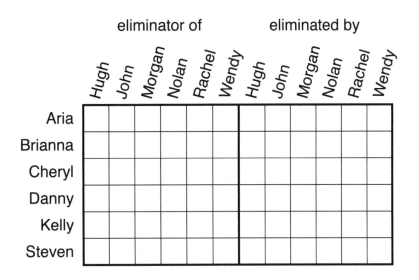

order of elimination

	1	2	3	4	5	6	7	8	9	10	11
Aria											
Brianna											
Cheryl											
Danny											
Kelly											
Steven											
Hugh											
John											
Morgan											
Nolan											
Rachel											
Wendy											

Sunday evening, not long before they are scheduled to leave the island, the visitors are sitting with the Montagues and the regular guests at the dining room table, which had been lengthened by the addition of a folding table. Just as everyone finishes dessert, a muffled crash is heard near the front of the house. Gordon, Nina, Taylor, and several of the others go to the front door and look outside.

Cheryl hangs back for a moment, having noticed that a visitor who had briefly left the table a few minutes earlier was still sitting. As she finally walks into the lounge, she watches in a wall mirror as the visitor switches empty water glasses with Gordon Montague and puts Gordon's glass into a bag.

In front of the house, a drone airplane less than two feet in length lies on the ground, one of its four propellers broken. Evidently it flew into the house.

"Who could have been flying this?" Nina wonders out loud. No one is in view.

"Someone in a nearby boat could have controlled it," you observe. "This is a quadcopter, equipped with a camera and video transmitter that could have been used to guide the drone through first-person view. Something like this can be controlled from up to a mile away, and as the crow flies we're only half a mile or so from the marina."

"But why? It doesn't seem to have done any real damage. A practice run?" Gordon speculates.

"Or a scare tactic, or a diversion of some kind," you offer. "These can fly more than 100 miles per hour, so even small ones like this are not harmless. I'll have it examined. These are supposed to be registered, but I doubt this one was."

An hour later, after the visitors have left the island, you address Gordon.

"That was quick thinking, asking the guests and their visitors to pose for a group photo out in the garden. After Cheryl told us what she had seen, I had time to find your glass in the luggage. Also thanks to Cheryl, I was able to replace it with a glass having the visitor's own fingerprints on it instead of yours."

"We don't want them to know we're onto them. But what should we do next?" Gordon asks.

"A couple of things," you reply. "We should search the mansion for anything the visitor might have hidden that would be inconvenient to have discovered by, say, law enforcement. And I need to keep a close eye on you in the next few days, which means that I'm going with you on your upcoming two-day meeting in Raleigh a week from Wednesday. I'll travel separately and keep my distance. During the evening at the hotel, I want you to be sure you are seen by several hotel employees and security cameras in case you need an alibi and my word isn't convincing enough. Whatever they plan to try, I think it will come during that time period, since it's unusual for you to be off the island on your own."

"But wouldn't that leave Cheryl and Nina less secure? I know my staff has some capability to defend the mansion, but you'd be an asset here."

"No, I think they've already accomplished whatever they wanted to do on the island, and anything important will take place in Raleigh, where my operative reports that Junior just rented a storefront. I'll tell my operative in Ojai, too, to stay alert."

Card-Jackers

The Montagues have written a mini-mystery suitable for the guests to act out and solve quickly after a late dinner.

The mansion is imagined to be hosting an auction of cards of all sorts—vintage baseball cards, rare cards from collectible card games such as Magic: The Gathering and Pokémon, and even antique decks of European playing cards. Before the auction, one or more of the would-be bidders, played by the guests, gained access to the private study where the cards were being kept and made off with the most valuable cards. From the statements of the Montagues and the guests, all of which were written by the Montagues, can you identify the thief or thieves?

Statements by the Montagues:

1. Gordon: Fewer than four of the guests were the thieves. As usual in our mysteries, every statement made by an innocent person is true, but a statement by a guilty person may be either true or false.

2. Nina: Neither Danny nor Brianna makes a true statement unless he or she is innocent.

Statements by the guests:

3. Aria: Either Brianna or Cheryl is guilty, but not both.

4. Brianna: Cheryl is innocent, and there were three thieves.

5. Cheryl: Steven is innocent, and there were three thieves.

6. Danny: Either Kelly or Steven is guilty, but not both.

7. Kelly: I am innocent, and there were two thieves.

8. Steven: I am innocent, and there were three thieves.

9. Taylor: Either Aria or Danny is lying, but not both.

Shady Shamuses

In this murder mystery, the guests and Nolan are playing members of the Shady Shamus Club, a group of private investigators so corrupt that each of them has investigated two of the others and been investigated by two of the others. Each of these detectives has been known to approach the target of an investigation and ask for a payoff in return for not reporting incriminating evidence to the detective's client.

The club is gathered for a recreational weekend at Montague Mansion. After dinner on Saturday, Nolan is found dead, having been given a fast-acting poison that anyone could have had the opportunity to administer. From the clues below, can you determine who the killer was, and also for what possible crime each of the club members had investigated other club members both five years ago and this year?

Statements by the Montagues:

1. Gordon: Each club member investigated one of the other members five years ago for a particular possible crime, and was investigating a different club member this year for a different possible crime. All the investigations referred to in any statement pertain to investigations of a club member by a club member.

2. Nina: Nolan was killed by a member he was currently investigating and who was also currently investigating Nolan. No guest makes a false statement.

Statements by the staff:

3. Alistair: Eight different possible crimes—blackmail, embezzlement, hiding assets, insurance fraud, money laundering, murder, tax evasion, and toxic waste dumping—were each investigated by a different club member five years ago, and the same eight crimes have been investigated again by eight different club members this year.

4. Charlotte: Five years ago, Nolan, Steven, and Taylor were investigating club members for the possible crimes of blackmail, embezzlement, and murder, in some combination.

5. Evelyn: Five years ago, Brianna, Cheryl, and Kelly were investigating club members for the possible crimes of hiding assets, tax evasion, and toxic waste dumping, in some combination.

6. Grant: This year, Brianna, Nolan, and Steven have been investigating club members for the possible crimes of blackmail, insurance fraud, and murder, in some combination.

7. Lyle: This year, the hiding assets investigation was aimed at the person who investigated hiding assets five years ago.

8. Sandy: This year's embezzlement investigator targeted the person who was investigating money laundering this year.

Statements by the guests:

9. Aria: Five years ago, Kelly, Steven, Taylor and I investigated one another, in some combination. This year, Brianna, Danny, and I have been investigating one another, in some combination.

10. Brianna: Five years ago, Kelly, Steven, and I were investigated by club members for insurance fraud, money laundering, and tax evasion, in some combination.

11. Cheryl: Five years ago I investigated the person who was then investigating money laundering.

12. Danny: This year, Cheryl, Kelly, and I have been investigated by club members for insurance fraud, money laundering, and tax evasion, in some combination.

13. Kelly: The person I investigated this year investigated a club member for murder five years ago.

14. Steven: Five years ago, I did not investigate blackmail.

15. Taylor: This year Cheryl and I have been investigating club members for the possible crimes of money laundering and tax evasion, not necessarily respectively.

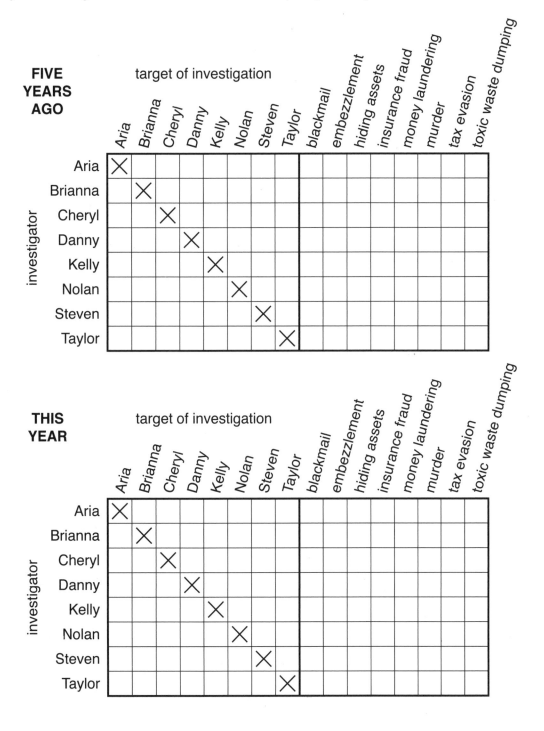

Curio Cabinet

The Montagues have a curio cabinet with 36 cubbyholes arranged in a 6×6 array. The also have a collection of 26 ceramic animals that are displayed in the curio cabinet, one animal per cubbyhole, with 10 cubbyholes remaining empty. From the clues below, can you determine how the animals are arranged within the cabinet?

1. The animals consist of 13 pairs of the following kinds: bat, cow, dolphin, fox, gorilla, jaguar, kiwi, monkey, ostrich, quail, sheep, vulture, zebu.

2. The third row from the top is the only row without an empty cubbyhole.

3. The letters of the alphabet A through Z can be found in order at the beginning or end of each animal's name, beginning with the first animal on the left in the top row and moving from left to right within each row, beginning with the top row and moving down. Thus, the first two animals are gorilla (for A) and bat (B), both of which are in the top row, and the last two animals are monkey (for Y) and zebu (Z), both of which are in the bottom row.

4. The kiwis are the only pair of matching animals that are in the same row.

5. A bat shares a column with one gorilla and a diagonal with the other gorilla.

6. The two diagonals that cross at one of the sheep's cubbyholes each contain an ostrich.

7. Nine matching pairs of animals share a column with each other, and every column contains at least one matching pair.

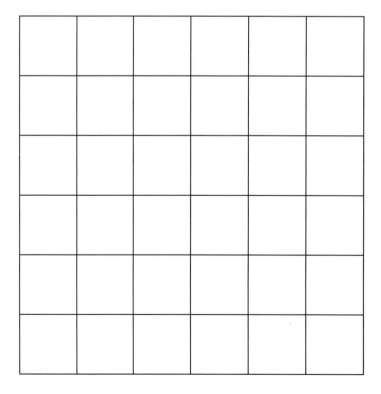

All the Marbles

"This is a warmup for a more elaborate puzzle I plan to present next weekend, using blocks," Gordon Montague tells the guests. "On this table are three groups of marbles. One pile contains three marbles, another five marbles, and the third pile eight marbles.

"I'm offering to play a game in which two players take turns removing any number of marbles they wish from any one group. The player who removes the last marble from the last remaining group wins.

"This is a mathematical game known as nim. If I give you the choice of moving first or second, which should you choose? And if you do move first, how many marbles should you remove, and from which group?

"Notice that if there are ever just two remaining groups with equal numbers of marbles, whoever moves next will lose. Because however many marbles the player removes from one group, the other player can remove the same number from the other group, until eventually that other player gets to remove the last marble."

You're on a street in Raleigh, North Carolina, on Monday afternoon. "That's the storefront I followed Junior to two weeks ago," your operative tells you, pointing through the coffee shop window to a building across the street from where you are sitting. "He was wearing a fake beard at the time, and paid two months' rent in cash. Some furniture has been delivered there since."

"Good work," you reply. "Keep an eye on the place each evening, especially this Wednesday night, and take photos of anyone who enters or leaves."

On Wednesday and Thursday, Gordon Montague attends a two-day board of directors meeting in Raleigh and stays at a local hotel Wednesday night.

On Friday, you update Gordon and Nina. "My operative following Kreuk reports he rented a boat the Sunday before last, so he is very likely the person who flew the drone into the house, timing it per instructions he got on his phone from the visitor. Yesterday, the police, FBI, and Secret Service all received anonymous tips about a Wednesday night poker game in which at least one player used counterfeit money. The caller named you, Gordon, and also accused you of having more counterfeit money hidden somewhere in your mansion. The scene of the alleged poker game was a back room in the storefront rented by Junior, and counterfeit money was in fact found there, evidently supplied by an old acquaintance of Kreuk's. But law enforcement had no trouble verifying that you were at your hotel that night, not at a poker game, and your fingerprint was not found on the water glass as the caller had promised. Someone else's was.

"Meanwhile, yesterday Linda received a suspicious package in the mail full of 20-dollar bills at her real estate office. She and turned it over to one of my Ojai operatives, who turned it over to authorities. All counterfeit. We haven't found anything hidden in the mansion yet, but I'm pretty sure we will."

Bridge Pros

In this role-playing puzzle, the goal is to discover which character is planning to kill which other character. The Montagues are acting the part of a wealthy couple who regularly hire professional bridge players to be on their team in knockout events at major tournaments. Bridge is a four-player card game in which players who sit across from one another, in directions conventionally called North-South and East-West, are partners. Knockout events involve teams of four that play a series of deals in which each set of hands is played twice, at two different tables. One team plays the North-South hands at one table and the East-West hands at the other table, and the results are later compared.

The Montagues will hire two pro pairs to play most of the tournament deals for the team, with the Montagues occasionally replacing one of the pairs so as to be able to share any title that the team wins. Six of the guests—Aria, Brianna, Cheryl, Danny, Kelly, and Steven—are assuming the roles of professional bridge players. Some of these pros have played as partners before. After a day of casual bridge with the pros at the mansion, the Montagues make known a list of their first nine choices for pairs of bridge partners, of which they will hire the top two pairs that consist of four different players (choosing the top pair, and then the highest-ranking pair that doesn't include either of those players) to compete in a major upcoming event. All nine pairs on the list are different combinations of the same six players.

Taylor, playing a security consultant, has information that one of the pros, who is not in the top two pairs on the Montagues' list, is planning to murder another player in order to move onto the team. The motive is a combination of greed (the Montagues pay very well) and a desire for prestige (the Montagues are often the winning team).

From the following clues assembled by Taylor, can you determine the bridge bidding systems used by each pro, the Montagues' rankings of the possible sets of bridge partners, the location where each such partnership had a major success during the past year, and which bridge player plans to kill which other player?

1. The six pros among themselves have formed nine different bridge partnerships during the past year, each of which won a major event in a different one of the following cities: Austin, Denver, Honolulu, Indianapolis, Las Vegas, Nashville, Phoenix, Pittsburgh, and St. Louis.

2. Three pros each use a different one of the following bidding systems: Standard American, Strong Club, and Two-Over-One (short for "2/1 game forcing"). The other three pros each play two of these systems, and no two play the same two systems. Two pros can only form a partnership if there is a bidding system that they both use.

3. The three Standard American bidders are Brianna, Kelly, and the player who partnered with Aria to win in Las Vegas.

4. One of the three Strong Club bidders won in Indianapolis but the other two—Cheryl and Danny—did not.

5. The three Two-Over-One bidders are Aria, Steven, and a player who won in Denver.

6. The top three pairs in the Montagues' rankings all include Kelly.

7. The bottom three pairs in the Montagues' rankings all include Steven.

8. Cheryl is part of pairs ranked 2nd, 4th, 6th, and 8th.

9. The pairs that won in Nashville, Phoenix, Pittsburgh, and St. Louis, are ranked 4th, 5th, 7th and 8th on the Montagues' list, not necessarily in that order.

10. The pair that won in Denver is ranked one place below the pair that won in Indianapolis.

11. The pair ranked 4th uses a Strong Club system.

12. The pair that won in Nashville is ranked higher than the team that won in Austin but lower than the pair that won in Pittsburgh.

13. The winning pairs in Nashville and St. Louis used the same bidding system.

14. The second-highest ranked pair that includes Brianna ranks higher than a pair that includes Kelly.

15. One of the four pros who are in the Montagues' most preferred pair of partnerships is the intended murder victim of one of the other two pros, who would be elevated to the Montagues' team if the murder is successful.

16. Of all the possible combinations of potential killers and victims that are consistent with clue 15, the would-be killer and victim are the pair that would result in the lowest possible sum of the rankings of the new pair of partnerships for the Montague team.

	1st	2nd	3rd	4th	5th	6th	7th	8th	9th	Std. American	Strong Club	Two-Over-One	Austin	Denver	Honolulu	Indianapolis	Las Vegas	Nashville	Phoenix	Pittsburgh	St. Louis
Aria																					
Brianna																					
Cheryl																					
Danny																					
Kelly																					
Steven																					
Austin													
Denver													
Honolulu													
Indianapolis													
Las Vegas													
Nashville													
Phoenix													
Pittsburgh													
St. Louis													
Std. American										
Strong Club										
Two-Over-One										

Bridge Amateurs

After playing the roles of bridge pros, the guests decide that although they are all novices, it might be fun to have an actual bridge tournament among themselves. The seven guests (Aria, Brianna, Cheryl, Danny, Kelly, Steven, and Taylor) and Nolan form four partnerships (pair 1, pair 2, pair 3, pair 4), which are then grouped into teams of four players three ways.

Eight deals were played during each of three matches. In the first match, pairs 1 and 2 formed a team against pairs 3 and 4; in the second match, pairs 1 and 3 formed a team against pairs 2 and 4; and in the third match, pairs 1 and 4 formed a team against pairs 2 and 3. In each match, the same hands were played by both teams and the results later compared.

For example, in the first round, pair 1 would play the North and South hands against pair 4 playing the East and West hands, and pair 2 (pair 1's teammates during that match) would play the East and West hands against pair 3 (pair 4's teammates) playing the North and South hands. If pair 1 scored 50 points with the North and South cards while pair 3 scored 120 points with the same North-South cards, the team of pairs 3 and 4 would have a net score of +70 on the hand. This number is then translated into International Match Points (IMPs) according to a standard scale from 1 to 24 points. The winner of a match is the team earning more IMPs than its opponent over the course of eight hands. Each team's margin of victory or loss in IMPs is scored by both pairs in the two partnerships. That is to say, the margin of victory in IMPs is awarded to each of the winning team's two partnerships, while the losing team's partnerships each receive the corresponding negative amount. After the three matches, each pair will have teamed up with every other pair, and the pair with the most net IMPs wins the tournament. For example, if a pair loses two matches by 5 IMPs each but also wins a match by 12 IMPs, it adds up its three scores (−5, −5, +12) to end the tournament with a net positive score of 2 IMPs.

From the clues below, can you determine who was partnered with whom, how many IMPs each team won or lost each of its three matches by, and what each pair's final score was?

1. Aria and her partner were outscored by their opponents by a total of 31 IMPs.

2. Brianna and her partner lost their third match.

3. Cheryl and her partner came in first despite losing their first match.

4. Danny and his partner lost their second match.

5. One of the winning players in the second match was Taylor.

6. Nolan and his partner won their third match and ended up outscoring their opponents by 13 IMPs.

7. Steven and his partner lost both their second and third matches.

8. Taylor's partnership was outscored by its opponents by just 1 IMP.

Knickknacks

The Montagues have a collection of whale knickknacks, nine of which are on display in several rooms in the mansion. Each is made of glass, metal, or wood and represents one of nine kinds of whales: beaked whale, beluga, blue whale, grey whale, humpback whale, narwhal, right whale, rorqual, and sperm whale.

From the clues below, can you determine the room in which each whale is on display and what material it is made of?

1. The dining room, private study, and sitting room each have one whale on display, and the library, the lounge, and the master bedroom each have two whales.

2. There are three glass whales, three metal whales, and three wooden whales. No room contains two whales made of the same material.

3. The glass whales are in the library, the master bedroom, and the private study.

4. There is no metal whale in the dining room or the library.

5. The blue whale, grey whale, and humpback whale are in the lounge, master bedroom, and sitting room, in some combination.

6. The narwhal, right whale, and rorqual are in the dining room, library, and private study, in some combination.

7. Neither the beaked whale nor the beluga, which are made of the same material, is in the master bedroom.

8. The blue whale and grey whale are made of the same material.

9. The narwhal and right whale are made of the same material.

10. The right whale, rorqual, and sperm whale are made of three different materials.

11. The other whales in the rooms with the beluga and sperm whales are made of the same material.

12. Neither the blue whale nor the narwhal shares a room with a wood whale.

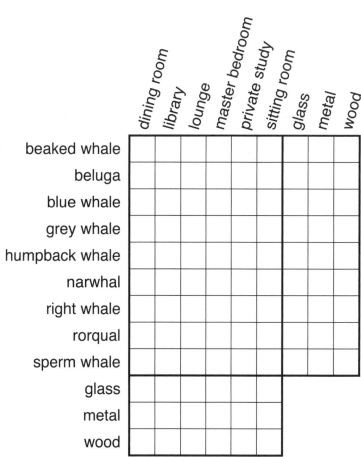

Mental Blocks

In the small game room, Gordon Montague has arranged some wooden blocks of varying sizes into seven groups. Except for the "group" consisting of a single block, blocks in each group are stacked into towers of various configurations, as shown, and labeled A through G.

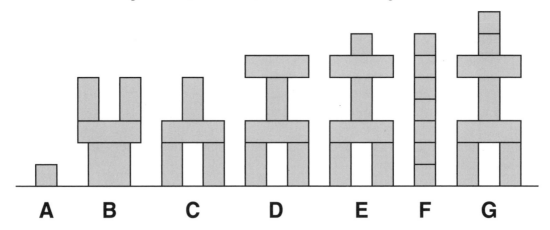

"Imagine a game in which you begin with three different block towers chosen from the seven that are on this table. I'm going to take the first turn, and then you and I will alternate. A turn consists of choosing one block in any of the three towers and removing that block, as well as any blocks that are above it in the same tower. The player who removes the last block from the last tower wins.

"For example, suppose we had simple towers of two, three, and four blocks. I would begin by removing the top three blocks from the tower of four, leaving groups of one, two, and three blocks. Now no matter what you did, I would be able to ensure that I get to take away the last block by creating two equal towers on my next turn. If you took away one block from the tower of three, for example, I would take away the single block, leaving two towers of two. If you then took away a block from one tower, I would take one from the other, leaving two single blocks. You would have to take one, so I would get to take the last one.

"To be clear about the rules, if you choose to remove one of the two bottom blocks from group C, for example, only the other bottom block would remain.

"I'm randomly assigning each of these groups of blocks to one of you. I assure you that there is no theoretical advantage or disadvantage in having any particular group." Gordon takes out seven index cards with the players' names on them, shuffles them, and deals each one face down next to a tower of blocks. Then he turns them over.

"Now that you know your block group, here is your difficult puzzle: Divide the other six guests into three pairs such that the two towers belonging to any one of the pairs, plus your tower, would be a winning combination of towers for you if we played the game I just described and I went first. There is a unique solution for each of you. I'll leave this set up over the weekend, so you can have until Sunday evening to solve it."

All the guests eventually solved the puzzle, so Gordon awarded competition points based on speed of solving. From the clues below, can you determine which guest had which group of blocks and the order in which the guests solved the puzzle? As a bonus, can you solve the puzzle yourself by finding the seven sets of three groups of blocks that will allow the guests to win if Gordon goes first?

1. The guests assigned block groups A, C, and G finished second, third, and fifth, in some combination.

2. The guests assigned block groups B, E, and F were Aria, Kelly, and Taylor, in some combination.

3. Kelly finished ahead of Steven but one place behind Brianna.

4. The guest assigned block group B finished ahead of the guest with block group E but behind the guest with block group F.

5. Kelly finished ahead of the guest who was assigned block group D.

6. Aria finished ahead of the guest who was assigned block group G but behind Danny.

7. Cheryl finished ahead of the guest who was assigned block group A.

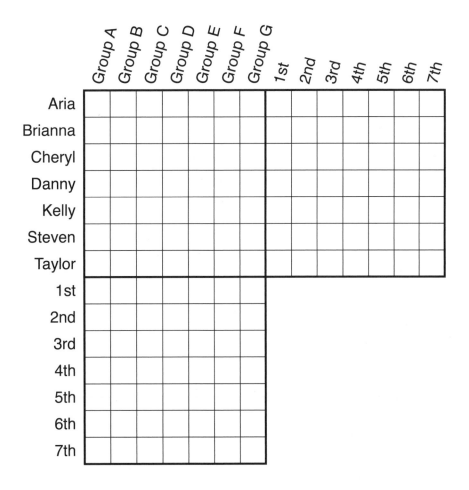

Endgame

Gordon has asked the guests to gather in the lounge.

"Some things have been going on that it's time for all of you to know about," he begins. "Cheryl will give you the details, but first a bit of background. Some 15 years ago I uncovered a massive fraud being perpetrated on investors by the well-known head of an investment fund. You may have heard of him—Felix Hochstapler. He has been in prison since, and until recently so was his son, Felix Jr., who was convicted on less serious charges and was released in late May. The Hochstaplers have threatened to one day get back at me for my role in exposing them. I guessed they might try to implicate me in some sort of crime, and we have finally learned their plan and notified the authorities."

Cheryl explains what they learned about the activities of Aiden Kreuk and Junior's activities, including the attempted switching of glasses by a visitor the night the drone hit the house.

"The Hochstaplers knew of my relation to Gordon, and so once Kreuk was released from prison in March, he began to look for someone who could get close enough to me to become a guest on the island. We suspect he may have placed a notice on the dark web to recruit people in their early-to-mid 20s living in the Raleigh-Durham area, so as to be near our law school—people who would be willing to do something underhanded for money.

"He may have initially hired more than one such person, and we may have all met them as they tried to get inside our circle of friends. At some point he learned of our plan to spend the summer on the island, and then his focus shifted to finding someone to befriend one of the five of you and possibly get an invitation to come here.

"Which did happen. Someone that one of you invited here two weeks ago was hired by Kreuk. Felix Jr. met with that person during a weekend in June to give them a down payment and instruct them on what to do here. I hope your relationship with them is only casual.

"In this island's tradition, I've made a puzzle that will reveal which of the five visitors you invited—Hugh, John, Morgan, Rachel, or Wendy—was on a mission for Felix Jr. It looks like that visitor will be testifying against Kreuk, who we hope in turn will testify against Junior."

1. During the four weekends of June, Felix Jr. and the five visitors—Hugh, John, Morgan, Rachel, and Wendy—each traveled to Delaware, Maryland, Pennsylvania, and Virginia, one state per weekend, in various sequences. At least one of these six people was present in each of the four states each weekend, and none of these people traveled to the same state twice.

2. Only once were the guilty visitor and Felix Jr. in the same state on the same weekend, and no other visitor was ever in the same state as Felix Jr. on the same weekend.

3. During weekend 1, Hugh, Morgan, and Wendy were not in Pennsylvania or Virginia.

4. During weekend 2, Hugh, Morgan, and Wendy were in Maryland, Pennsylvania, and Virginia, in some combination, and the same was true during weekend 3.

5. During weekend 4, Hugh, John, Morgan, and Rachel were not in Maryland or Pennsylvania.

6. John was in Pennsylvania later than he was in Maryland.

7. Rachel was in Pennsylvania one weekend later than she was in Maryland but earlier than she was in Virginia.

8. Hugh and John were in the same state during weekend 2.

	Weekend 1				Weekend 2				Weekend 3				Weekend 4			
	DE	MD	PA	VA	DE	MD	PA	VA	DE	MD	PA	VA	DE	MD	PA	VA
Felix Jr.																
Hugh																
John																
Morgan																
Rachel																
Wendy																

Arrangements

Gordon and Nina Montague are visiting Cheryl's parents, Kirk and Linda, at their home in Ojai. Cheryl, Nolan, and Taylor are also present to celebrate the end of the Hochstapler problem.

"It's official now," Gordon remarks, "Kreuk has agreed to testify against Felix Jr. Charges will include making false statements to both local and federal law enforcement, when they made anonymous calls to report that I was passing off counterfeit money at a poker game. After the fingerprint on the glass was identified, Junior, Kreuk, and Kreuk's accomplice ended up being the ones charged with distributing counterfeit money. After obtaining the counterfeit bills from an old acquaintance of Kreuk's, they had planted some in the poker room, mailed some to Linda's office, and hidden some in our library, which we eventually found. The person who rented out the storefront to Junior wasn't able to make a positive identification, but it didn't matter since Taylor's operative can connect Junior to the poker room with testimony and photos. So we won't have Junior to worry about anymore.

"And congratulations are in order to Cheryl, not only for making a key observation that helped resolve this matter, but also for being the most efficient puzzle solver of all the guests over the course of the summer."

"Thank you, Grandpa," Cheryl replies with a smile. "And now I have an announcement for everyone, one that I've already shared with Grandpa, since it means he needs to find a new pilot for his boat and helicopter. Nolan is going to follow me to New York when I start my new job."

Kirk and Linda are clearly very happy about the news. People chat about what sort of job Nolan would look for in New York, what Cheryl's Manhattan apartment—which her law firm found for her over the summer while she was on the island—was like, and how long Cheryl would need to work at the law firm before being able to take a vacation. Cheryl and Nolan leave the impression that they may soon announce their engagement, but Cheryl hints that she first wants to be sure that the New York law firm is a good long-term fit.

Linda slips away from the group and returns with a poster board on which are mounted 12 photos of a baby girl labeled A through L.

"Knowing how you all like puzzles, I thought I'd give you this challenge: Arrange these photos of Cheryl in chronological order. They were taken roughly a month apart between the day she was born and her first birthday, but are now in random order. Cheryl and Nolan have seen these before, so it's up to the rest of you to take your best guesses. After your guesses, Cheryl will give you clues about how close you came, and from that information I expect you will be able to determine the correct solution."

Gordon, Nina, and Taylor independently assign each photo a number from 1 through 12 based on whether they think it came first (1), last (12), or somewhere in between. The guesses, written down for all to see, were as follows:

	A	B	C	D	E	F	G	H	I	J	K	L
Gordon	1	7	3	10	5	4	12	8	9	6	2	11
Nina	2	7	5	12	3	9	11	6	8	4	1	10
Taylor	3	9	2	11	4	5	10	8	12	6	1	7

After studying the guesses, Cheryl makes the following remarks:

"Grandpa, two of your guesses are correct, four are one higher than the correct number, four are one lower than the correct number, one is two higher than the correct number, and one is two lower than the correct number.

"Nina, two of your guesses are correct, two are one higher than the correct number, five are one lower than the correct number, one is two higher than the correct number, one is two lower than the correct number, and one is three higher than the correct number.

"Taylor, three of your guesses are correct, four are one higher than the correct number, two are one lower than the correct number, one is two higher than the correct number, and two are two lower than the correct number."

What is the correct order of the photos?

ANSWERS AND EXPLANATIONS

Note: Throughout these answers, numbered statements in the puzzles are referred to as "clues."

Early Spring

Ojai Puzzle 1: Toppings

Andrew ordered black olives, mushrooms, and peppers.
Cheryl ordered broccoli, mushrooms, and onions.
Gordon ordered artichokes, onions, and peppers.
Kirk ordered black olives, onions, and spinach.
Linda ordered artichokes, black olives, and broccoli.
Nina ordered artichokes, mushrooms, and spinach.
Taylor ordered broccoli, peppers, and spinach.

From clues 2 and 6, Kirk had a topping that was also ordered by Nina and Taylor, since Kirk already had a topping in common with each of the other people. From the eliminations in clues 3, 4, and 5, this topping was spinach.

From clue 7 and the above eliminations, the topping that Gordon, Linda, and Nina all ordered was artichokes. By elimination, Cheryl ordered broccoli, mushrooms, and onions. The topping that Cheryl, Gordon, and Kirk all ordered (clue 6) was onions.

The topping ordered by Cheryl, Linda, and Taylor (clue 8) cannot be mushrooms, since Andrew ordered that (clue 9), and so it was broccoli. By elimination, Nina had mushrooms and Andrew had black olives and peppers. Since Linda did not have peppers (clue 10), the topping that Kirk and Linda had in common was black olives (clue 6). Gordon and Taylor ordered peppers.

Weekend 1

Puzzle 1.1: Starting Out

Aria interned in Los Angeles for Cash & Carey.
Brianna interned in Chicago for Hunt & Peck.
Cheryl interned in New York City for Hart & Soul.
Danny interned in Washington for Black & White.
Kelly interned in San Antonio for Dey & Knight.
Steven interned in Atlanta for Hale & Hardy.

From clue 1, Neither Aria nor Brianna interned at Hale & Hardy, and neither they nor the Hale & Hardy intern will be working in New York City, San Antonio, or Washington.

From clue 2, Cheryl did not intern with Black & White or Dey & Knight, and neither she nor those interns will be working in Atlanta, Chicago, or Los Angeles. Since are those are the only possible cities for Aria and Brianna to have interned, neither of them interned with Black & White or Dey & Knight. For the same reason, Cheryl did not intern with Hale & Hardy.

From clue 3, Danny did not intern with Hart & Soul or Hunt & Peck, and none of those three students interned in Atlanta, Los Angeles, or San Antonio.

From clue 4, Steven did not intern at Cash & Carey, and neither Steven nor the Cash & Carey intern worked in Chicago, New York City, San Antonio, or Washington.

Since Black & White, Dey & Knight, Hart & Soul, and Hunt & Peck are not located in Atlanta or Los Angeles, Steven did not intern with any of those firms, and by elimination interned with Hale & Hardy, which is therefore not in Chicago. Since Cash & Carey is not located in any of the cities where Cheryl or Danny

could have worked, they did not intern with Cash & Carey. From clue 7, Cheryl did not intern at Hunt & Peck, and by elimination interned at Hart & Soul.

Since Kelly interned in either Los Angeles or San Antonio (clue 5), Kelly did not intern at Hunt & Peck. The interns at Black & White and Dey & Knight, then, can only be Danny and Kelly in some combination, which means that Kelly did not intern at Cash & Carey. Since neither Black & White nor Dey & Knight is in Los Angeles or Chicago, Kelly must have interned in San Antonio and Danny did not intern in Chicago.

From clue 6, Cheryl, who interned at Hart & Soul, did not intern in Washington, so her internship was in New York City. By elimination, Danny was in Washington.

Since Dey & Knight is not in Washington (clue 6), Danny's Washington internship was at Black & White, and by elimination Kelly's San Antonio internship was at Dey & Knight.

From clue 8, Brianna did not intern at Cash & Carey, so Aria did, and since she wasn't in Chicago, she was in Los Angeles. By elimination, Brianna interned at Hunt & Peck in Chicago, and Steven's Hale & Hardy internship was in Atlanta.

Puzzle 1.2: The Purloined Necklaces

Cheryl and Steven are the thieves. Cheryl stole the pearl necklace from Charlotte's room and Steven stole the diamond necklace from the master bedroom.

The statements of Cheryl and Steven contradict one another, and so one of them is lying and is guilty, per clue 2.

Danny's statement means either that Danny is lying or that either Aria or Cheryl is guilty.

Taylor's statement means either that Taylor is lying or that either Danny or Steven is guilty.

Danny's and Taylor's statements cannot both be false, because that would mean they as well as either Cheryl or Steven are guilty, contradicting Alistair's statement that there were at most two thieves. Both statements could be true, or one could be true and the other false.

If Danny's statement is false, then Danny is guilty and Taylor's statement is true. The other guilty party is either Cheryl or Steven, as determined previously.

If Taylor's statement is false, then Taylor is guilty and Danny's statement is true. In that case, either Aria or Cheryl is guilty; but the guilty party would have to be Cheryl, since either she or Steven is guilty.

Since Aria, Brianna, and Kelly are not possible thieves, they are innocent and their statements can be trusted. The statements of Brianna, Kelly, Grant, and Lyle exonerate Danny and Taylor, making their statements trustworthy. Cheryl's statement was true, but she and Steven are the guilty parties.

Puzzle 1.3: Menagerie

The animal sculptures are at the following locations: bear–old well, cougar–pond, deer–mansion, eagle–Lookout Point, fox–old hut, groundhog–windmill, otter–boathouse, raccoon–bridge, tortoise–sea caves, wolf–lighthouse.

Since the six animal sculptures mentioned in clues 1 and 2 will account for all six sculpture locations that are north of the mansion and/or east of the old well, the other four sculptures—bear, deer, otter, and wolf—are at the boathouse, lighthouse, mansion, and old well in some combination. From clue 3 and the distance table, the deer and otter are at the boathouse and mansion in some order, and so the bear and wolf are at the lighthouse and old well in some order.

From clue 2, the eagle is in one of the four locations east of the old well. From clue 4, if the eagle is at the old hut or the windmill, the equal distances to the pond and sea caves would not provide a location the otter can be, whereas the equal distances to the mansion and Lookout Point would not provide a possible location for the fox (which is farther north than the mansion, per clue 1). If the eagle is at the sea caves, the otter could be at the mansion and the fox at the old hut, both of which are 8 units of distance from the sea caves. If the eagle is at Lookout Point, the otter could be at either the boathouse or the mansion and the fox could be at the old hut. In each of these cases, the fox is at the old hut, so that is its location. That eliminates one of the locations east of the old well, so the other three are accounted for by the animals in clue 2, and the cougar and raccoon are not at the windmill.

The raccoon now has two possible locations. If the raccoon is at the pond, however, no pair of equidistant locations are possible for the eagle and wolf (clue 5). Therefore the raccoon is at the bridge, the eagle is at Lookout Point, and the wolf is at the lighthouse, which means that the bear is at the old well. By elimination, the cougar is at the pond.

From clue 6 and the fact that the mansion and the sea caves are the same distance from the pond, the deer is at the mansion and the tortoise is at the sea caves. By elimination, the otter is at the boathouse and the groundhog is at the windmill.

Weekend 2

Puzzle 2.1: Chez Thérèse

Aria ordered avocado cocktail, Caesar salad, filet mignon, and chocolate mousse.
Brianna ordered hearts of palm, soup du jour, gnocchi champignons, and crème brûlée.
Cheryl ordered avocado cocktail, French onion soup, poulet à la lavande, and chocolate mousse.
Danny ordered chef's mussels, soup du jour, saumon à l'orange, and cheesecake.
Gordon ordered escargots, beet salad, gnocchi champignons, and crème brûlée.
Kelly ordered hearts of palm, Caesar salad, poulet à la lavande, and cheesecake.
Nina ordered avocado cocktail, soup du jour, gnocchi champignons, and crème brûlée.
Nolan ordered avocado cocktail, beet salad, poulet à la lavande, and opera torte.
Steven ordered hearts of palm, soup du jour, gnocchi champignons, and crème brûlée.
Taylor ordered escargots, Caesar salad, saumon à l'orange, and cheesecake.

From clues 2, 3, and 10, the only person ordering chef's mussels was Danny. (Each of the four ordered one item no one else ordered; none of those items can have been from the same course, so there was one per course. Since Aria, Cheryl, and Nolan all had avocado cocktail, Danny must have been the person who was the only one to order mussels.) Aria, Cheryl, and Nolan can't have been the only three to order avocado cocktail, because if three people ordered any item, Kelly must have been one of them (clue 7). Therefore a fourth person ordered avocado cocktail, and it must have been Nina (clue 6).

From clue 5, Kelly ordered beet salad or Caesar salad, which means, per clue 7, that one of those was ordered by two other people (that is, three people in total). Three people can't have ordered beet salad, though, since more people ordered hearts of palm than beet salad (clue 13), and we've already accounted for the hors d'oeuvre ordered by four people. Kelly and two others therefore ordered Caesar salad, and the other two people who ordered salad had beet salad, which means three people ordered hearts of palm and two ordered escargots. Brianna, Kelly, and Steven ordered the same hors d'oeuvre (clues 8 and 10), so they must have been the three who had hearts of palm, and by elimination Gordon and Taylor had escargots.

From clue 9, at least three people ordered soup du jour; from clue 2 and the fact that three people ordered Caesar salad, soup du jour can't also have been ordered by three people, so four people ordered soup du jour. From clue 6, Nina ordered soup du jour, and from clue 9, she must also have ordered gnocchi champignons and crème brûlée, since each of those was ordered by four people. By elimination, one person ordered French onion soup. We already know Danny's order of chef's mussels was ordered by no one else. Of the group who ordered soup (all those not mentioned in clue 5), the only other one who had an item no one else ordered was Cheryl (clue 3), so she ordered the French onion soup and Brianna, Danny, and Steven are the others who had soup du jour.

From clues 2 and 4, poulet à la lavande was ordered by three people, which means that Kelly was one of them (clue 7) and Gordon was not (clue 12). Gordon, then, ordered gnocchi champignons (clue 4) and also crème brûlée (clue 9). Since Cheryl's avocado cocktail was ordered by three other people, from clue 3 she cannot be part of the group of four who ordered gnocchi champignons and therefore ordered poulet à la lavande. Since Brianna and Steven ordered the same things (clue 8), they had the other two orders of gnocchi champignons. Of the three people in clue 4, Aria must be the one who had the item no one else ordered (since Danny already ordered such an item, and Taylor never did). Two people ordered saumon à l'orange and cheesecake (clue 15), so Aria ordered filet mignon, and Danny and Taylor were the two who ordered saumon à l'orange and cheesecake. By elimination, Nolan ordered poulet à la lavande.

Three of Danny's orders are accounted for, so by elimination his dessert, cheesecake, must have been ordered by a total of three people. Kelly, then, was the other person to order it (clue 7). Since Danny didn't order Caesar salad, the other person besides Kelly who ordered cheesecake, Taylor, must have done so (clue 14).

Aria and Cheryl ordered chocolate mousse (clue 11), and since the dessert items ordered by three and four people are accounted for, they were the only two. The item Nolan alone ordered, then, can only be opera torte, and by elimination, Brianna and Steven ordered crème brûlée.

Three of Aria's orders are accounted for, so her salad, by elimination, must have been the one ordered by three people. She therefore had the Caesar salad, and by elimination, Gordon and Nolan ordered beet salad.

Puzzle 2.2: On Broadway

Aria's list has the songs "Cabaret," "Memory," "Ol' Man River," "People," and "Tonight."
Brianna's list has the songs "Cabaret," "Maria," "Memory," "Tomorrow," and "Tonight."
Cheryl's list has the songs "Cabaret," "Maria," "Memory," "People," and "Tonight."
Danny's list has the songs "Aquarius," "Cabaret," "Memory," "Ol' Man River," and "People."

Kelly's list has the songs "Aquarius," "If I Loved You," "Mame," "Maria," and "Tonight."

Steven's list has the songs "Mame," "Maria," "Memory," "Tomorrow," and "Tonight."

Taylor's list has the songs "Aquarius," "Cabaret," "Mame," "Memory," and "People."

The number of lists each song is on are: "Aquarius," 3; "Cabaret," 5; "If I Loved You," 1; "Mame," 3; "Maria," 4; "Memory," 6; "Ol' Man River," 2; "People," 4; "Tomorrow," 2; and "Tonight," 5.

From clues 1 and 3, "Aquarius" and "Mame" are both on two, three, four, or five lists. Between them, then, they fully account for one of those numbers of lists, so the relationships in clue 2 can only be true if the only song that is on six lists is "Cabaret" or "Memory," and if the song on just one list is "If I Loved You" or "Ol' Man River." From clue 2, "Cabaret" and "Memory" appear on at least four lists, "Maria" and "Tonight" are on at least three, "If I Loved You" and "Ol' Man River" appear on at most three lists, and "Tomorrow" and "People" are on at most four lists.

From clue 4, "Mame" is not on four or five lists. From clue 7, "Cabaret" does not appear on six lists, and so "Memory" does. From clue 8, the list on which "Memory" does not appear is either Danny's or Kelly's, and so "Memory" appears on all the other lists.

From clue 8, one of the songs on Danny's list is either "Maria" or "Memory," and so from clues 4 and 6, the five songs on Danny's list include "Aquarius," "Cabaret," "Ol' Man River," and "People."

From clues 5 and 9, "Aquarius" is on fewer than five lists. Since "Cabaret" appears on more lists than "Maria" (clue 2), "Maria" appears on fewer than five lists, and the two five-list songs (per clue 1) are "Cabaret" and "Tonight." From clue 7, "Cabaret" is on all the lists except Kelly's and Steven's; from clue 6, "Tonight" is on all the lists except Danny's and Taylor's.

Since "Tonight" appears on both Aria's and Kelly's lists, "Memory" cannot (clue 11). Therefore, from clue 8, "Maria" appears on Kelly's list and "Memory" appears on Danny's.

From clue 12 and the eliminations in clues 4, 5, and 7, the other songs that are on both Brianna's and Steven's lists (besides "Memory" and "Tonight," which we already know) must be "Maria" and "Tomorrow." Therefore, Aria's list has "People" but not "Tomorrow" (clue 10), and "Aquarius" is on Taylor's list but not Steven's (clue 9).

Since "Aquarius" and "Mame" are on the same number of lists (clue 3), but "Mame" is not on four lists (clue 4), "Aquarius" is not on four lists. Therefore, from clue 13, "Tomorrow" is on two lists (Brianna's and Steven's only), and "Aquarius" and "Mame" are each on three lists. "Mame" is therefore on the lists of Kelly, Steven, and Taylor, per clue 4. By elimination, "Maria" and "People" are on four lists each, and so "People" is on Cheryl's and Taylor's lists (it's not on Kelly's, per clue 7). All five songs on Steven's and Taylor's lists are now accounted for. "If I Loved You" is on neither Steven's nor Taylor's list and is only on Kelly's list (clue 4).

Since "If I Loved You" is on just one list, "Ol' Man River" is on two. "Ol' Man River" is on Aria's list (per the eliminations in clues 5 and 7) so "Aquarius" and "Maria" are not; "Aquarius" is on Kelly's list (clue 5), and "Maria" is on Cheryl's list.

Puzzle 2.3: Double 9 Special

Tile X is 1-9, tile Y is 4-7, and tile Z is 1-3.

Since Player C has three 9's and Player A has no 9's or matching sets of pips, Player A's hand can only be better than C's if tiles X and Y yield either a straight or a Special. The straight could not be 9 high, since it would then lose to Player C's four 9's. Any other

straight would have to contain a 4, but in that case Player E would have four 4's, and Player A would not be first. Therefore, Player A has a Special, and dominoes X and Y must together have the pips 1, 4, 7, and 9. Since dominoes 1-4, 4-9, and 7-9 are in players' hands, dominoes X and Y must be 1-9 and 4-7 in some combination.

Since one of these dominoes has a 9, Player C will have four 9's when whichever of the tile pairs X and Z or Y and Z that includes a 9 is added to the players' hands. Despite that, Player C loses to Player B both times, which means that Player B had to have five 1's to beat the four 9's. Domino Z therefore contains a 1.

When domino Z (1-?) is paired with the 4-7 domino, Player E will have four 4's. This beats a holding of four 1's by Player B, so the 4-7 domino must be domino Y (since player E loses to player B in the X-Z hand), and the 1-9 domino is domino X. We still don't know the missing digit on domino Z.

When domino Z is paired with the 1-9 domino, Player E has a full house of 4's and 1's, yet loses to Player D's set of tiles. D must have a higher full house, which means that domino Z is 1-3 or 1-0. Since 1-0 is in Player B's hand, it is 1-3.

With dominoes X and Y added to all hands, Player A has a Special, C has four 9's, E has four 4's, B has four 1's, and D has three 9's.

With dominoes X and Z added to all hands, Player B has five 1's, C has four 9's, D has a full house of 9's and 3's, E has a full house of 4's and 1's, and A has a pair of 3's.

With dominoes Y and Z added to all hands, Player E has four 4's, B has four 1's, A has a straight (0 through 4), C has three 9's, and D has three 3's.

Puzzle 2.4: Alibis

The killers are Brianna and Kelly.

Aria is the designer.
Brianna is the financier.
Cheryl is the clerk.
Danny is the actuary
Kelly is the beekeeper.
Steven is the electrician.
Taylor is the geologist.

Since Danny, Kelly, Steven, and Taylor were together from 3 P.M. to 5 P.M. on Saturday (per Danny, Kelly, and Taylor's statements), which according to Alistair's statement is the time when the first murder occurred, Uncle Barney's killer was Aria, Brianna, or Cheryl.

From 1 to 2 on Sunday Cheryl says she was with Aria and the beekeeper while Aria says she was with the clerk and the beekeeper; therefore, Cheryl is the clerk. From 2 to 3 on Sunday, Aria says she was with the actuary and financier, while Brianna says she was with the actuary and designer; therefore, Aria is the designer and Brianna is the financier. Since Kelly says she was with the designer from 1 to 2 on Sunday, she was the third person with Aria and Cheryl that hour and is the beekeeper.

From Danny's statement, he is not the electrician or geologist, and so by elimination is the actuary. From Brianna's statement, Steven is not the geologist, and so by elimination, Steven is the electrician and Taylor is the geologist.

According to Sandy, Danny was in the library from 1 to 2 on Sunday. The other guests each claim to have been with two other guests that hour. From their statements and known occupations, Aria, Cheryl, and Kelly were walking together, and Brianna, Steven, and Taylor were walking together. The murder could not have taken place that hour.

According to Sandy, Brianna was in the library from 3 to 4 on Sunday. From their statements and known occupations, Cheryl, Danny, and Kelly were together in the lounge from 3 to 4. Aria, Steven, and Taylor's statements confirm that they were walking together from 3 to 4. The murder could not have taken place that hour.

Between 2 and 3, Aria, Brianna, and Danny were together, and so were Cheryl, Steven, and Taylor. Kelly claims to have been with two other guests, but was lying and used that hour to kill Uncle Charlie.

Kelly's accomplice was Aria, Brianna, or Cheryl. Since Kelly was with Aria from 1 to 2 and with Cheryl from 3 to 4, clue 5 means that Aria and Cheryl are innocent.

Weekend 3

Puzzle 3.1: At the Sea Caves

For each set of statements, consider each possible prize location and which statements would be true or false in each case.

The answers are 1-B, 2-C, 3-A, 4-B, 5-C, 6-A, 7-B, 8-A. (In puzzle 7, when the prize is in Cave B, two statements are true, while only one statement is true if the prize is in Cave A or C. In puzzle 8, If you know there is one true statement, the prize could be in B or C. If you know there are two true statements, the prize is in A, so that's where the prize must be. It's not possible for there to be zero or three true statements.) Cave C is the answer to the fewest questions and is the location of the prize.

Puzzle 3.2: Trivia Tic-Tac-Toe

The X team consisted of Aria, Brianna, and Danny, who played in that sequence. The O team consisted of Cheryl, Kelly, and Steven, who played in that order.

The O team won by virtue of giving 10 correct answers, one more than the X team. If Brianna had answered her last question correctly, her team would have won,

The game played out as follows:

1. Aria incorrect, Cheryl correct, Kelly incorrect, Brianna correct (captures square for X)
2. Steven correct, Cheryl correct, Kelly incorrect, Danny incorrect, Steven correct (captures square for O)
3. Aria correct, Brianna correct, Danny correct (captures square for X)
4. Cheryl correct, Kelly correct (captures square for O)
5. Aria incorrect, Steven incorrect, Brianna correct (captures square for X)
6. Cheryl correct, Kelly correct (captures square for O)
7. Danny correct, Aria correct (captures square for X)
8. Steven incorrect, Brianna incorrect, Cheryl correct (captures square for O)
9. Danny correct, Aria correct, Brianna incorrect, Kelly correct (captures square for O, but more importantly gives O a 10–9 edge in correct answers)

Call the first X player to answer a question X1, the next one X2, and the last one X3; and call the first O player to answer a question O1, the next one O2, and the last one O3.

From clue 1, the first square began with an incorrect answer by X1. This was followed by either an incorrect answer by O1 and a correct answer by X2, or by a correct answer by O1, an incorrect

answer by O2, and a correct answer by X2 (with an extra question having been added). From clue 8, there could not have been more incorrect answers in that square.

Since X won the first square, the second square began with a question answered by an O team player. Since five questions were answered there (clue 8), the next-to-last question was answered incorrectly by an X player. The four possible sequences in the center square are:

1. O incorrect, X3 correct, X1 correct, X2 incorrect, O correct
2. O correct, O incorrect, X3 correct, X1 incorrect, O correct
3. O correct, O correct, O incorrect, X3 incorrect, O correct
4. O incorrect, X3 incorrect, O incorrect, X1 incorrect, O correct

If the first square had gone X1 incorrect, O1 incorrect, X2 correct, the only sequence in the center square in which there would be three questions between O1's two questions, as required by clue 9, is scenario 3. But in that case, there would have been more than three questions between O3's first two questions. Therefore, the first square sequence was an incorrect answer by X1, a correct answer by O1, an incorrect answer by O2, and a correct answer by X2. The possible center square sequences now look like this:

1. O3 incorrect, X3 correct, X1 correct, X2 incorrect, O1 correct
2. O3 correct, O1 incorrect, X3 correct, X1 incorrect, O2 correct
3. O3 correct, O1 correct, O2 incorrect, X3 incorrect, O3 correct
4. O3 incorrect, X3 incorrect, O1 incorrect, X1 incorrect, O2 correct

Of these possibilities, the only one in which there are three questions between O1's and O2's first two questions is the third sequence, so it must be the correct one.

Given that X answered the first question on the third square and won the square, and that there were no more than four questions answered there (per clue 8), there are three possibilities of how the questions in the third square could have been answered:

1. X1 correct, X2 correct, X3 correct
2. X1 incorrect, O1 incorrect, X2 correct
3. X1 incorrect, O1 correct, O2 incorrect, X2 correct

Per clue 9, there were six questions answered between O1's second and third answers, which eliminates all but the first option, so X1, X2, and X3 all gave correct answers in that square.

To fulfill the "six questions" condition of clue 9, the next four answers must be answered by O, O, X, and O, respectively. This can be accomplished in two ways:

1. If O1 and O2 both answer correctly on square 4 followed by an incorrect first answer on square 5 by X1
2. If square 4's answers are: O1 correct, O2 incorrect, X1 incorrect, O3 correct

If option 2 is correct, that means two additional questions were used on that square besides the original two. But let's consider: square 1 and square 2 have each had an additional question already, and an additional question will also be used on square 9 (per clue 10). There are 24 questions to start with on the board, and a total of 28 questions were answered in the game (per clue 7). The questions on the board plus the three additional questions we already know about accounts for 27 questions, so there can't be two additional questions on square 4, which means option 1 must be correct.

On square 5, since the square ended up with an X, O3 must have also given a wrong answer, after which X2 captured the square. Also, since O3's wrong answer causes an additional question to be used on this square, that question plus the three we know about accounts for all the additional questions, and so no additional questions are used on squares 6, 7, and 8.

Squares 6 and 7 were won by the team who answered the first question, so O1 and O2 both answered correctly on square 6 and X3 and X1 answered correctly on square 7. (Any other outcome would add a question, which we've shown is impossible.) Counting up all the answers so far, that leaves 4 answers for the X team and 3 answers for the O team.

On square 8, O answered the first and last questions, and on square 9, O answered the last question. That accounts for all of O's remaining answers, so all the other questions were answered by X. Square 8, then, must have been: O3 incorrect, X2 incorrect, O1 correct. On square 9, it was: X3 correct, X1 correct, X2 incorrect, O2 correct.

Going back through the game, we see that the number of correct answers, incorrect answers, and squares captured for each player are as follows:

X1: 3 correct, 2 incorrect, 1 square captured
X2: 3 correct, 2 incorrect, 2 squares captured
X3: 3 correct, 1 incorrect, 1 square captured
O1: 5 correct, 0 incorrect, 1 square captured
O2: 3 correct, 2 incorrect, 3 squares captured
O3: 2 correct, 2 incorrect, 1 square captured

Clues 3, 4, 5, and 6 pinpoint Brianna as X2, Danny as X3, Kelly as O2, and Steven as O3. From clue 2, Aria is X1 and Cheryl is O1.

Puzzle 3.3: Mansion Meanders

Aria began in the library and took four minutes by going through the art gallery, foyer, stairs, and second-floor hall to reach the sitting room.

Brianna began in basement 2 and took five minutes by going through the tunnel under the staff wing, the secret passage, the closet in staff room S5, staff room S5, and the second-floor hallway to reach the sitting room. (Using the tunnel under the guest wing and going through guest room 2B or 2C's closet would have been equally fast, but Brianna never entered the guest wing, per clue 4.)

Cheryl began in the game alcove and took two minutes by going to the small game room and second-floor hall to reach the sitting room.

Danny began in the wine cellar and took four minutes by going to basement 1, the adjacent storage area, the secret passage, and the closet off the sitting room to reach the sitting room.

Kelly began in guest room 1A and took three minutes by going to the first-floor hall, the guest wing stairs, and the second-floor hall to reach the sitting room. (Using the foyer stairs would have been equally fast but would contradict clue 4.)

Steven began in the master bath and took four minutes by going to the master bedroom, the third-floor hall, the stairs, and the second-floor hall to reach the sitting room. (Using the secret passage via the closet off the master bedroom would have been equally fast but would contradict clue 2, since Danny used a secret passage.)

Taylor began in the big game room and took one minute by taking the second-floor hall to the sitting room.

Puzzle 3.4: Footsteps

Taylor is the killer.

From clue 8, the foyer stairs were used nine times, but the guests only admit using them a total of seven times (three times by Aria and once each by Cheryl, Danny, Kelly, and Taylor). One of the guests took the foyer stairs two extra times, is lying, and is therefore the killer.

In view of clue 7, the statements of Brianna and Steven can be trusted, since if they lied about taking the guest wing stairs, there would be at least two liars, contradicting Nina's statement that there is only one killer.

From the starting and ending locations of the seven guests (which clue 2 assures us are true), four went down a floor and three went up a floor between 10 A.M. and 11 A.M. If Aria lied and is the one who made two extra trips, then Steven's statement is true and Aria didn't leave the room until four other trips had been made on the foyer stairs, which means the remaining five trips on the foyer stairs would all have been made by her. But clue 6 proves that the last two foyer stair trips were made by different people, and so Aria is telling the truth. Therefore, after the first five trips on the stairs that Aria heard, she went up, down, and up the stairs, and was followed by one other person going up, which had to be Danny, since the only other person who ended up on the second floor was Steven, who took the guest wing stairs earlier.

Since the last four trips on the foyer stairs were up-down-up-up, to fulfill Evelyn's statement in clue 5, one of the three people who went from the second floor to the first floor via the foyer stairs (Cheryl, Kelly, and Taylor) must have used the foyer stairs two extra times, going down-up-down, and the first five trips on the stairs had to have the order down-down-up-down-down. Whoever was the second person down the foyer stairs was the person who went back up and then down again without anyone else using those stairs in between (clue 3), followed by the fifth person that Aria heard on the stairs, who was going down.

Taylor left guest room 2A before Kelly left the big game room (Kelly's and Taylor's statements agree about the order in which they arrived in the lounge), and after Cheryl left the big game room (clue 4); Cheryl was therefore the first of the three to use the foyer stairs. Per Brianna's, Kelly's, and Taylor's statements, Taylor reached the lounge first, then Kelly, and then Brianna. Since Taylor used the foyer stairs before Kelly did, Taylor was the second person to use the stairs and is the killer.

As for the rest of the guests' movements, Brianna heard Steven on the guest wing stairs after the first four foyer stairs trips (by Cheryl and Taylor), which Steven had heard, had taken place. In the lounge, Brianna heard only the last four uses of the foyer stairs. Therefore, she went downstairs after Kelly did but before Aria. Kelly was the fifth person Aria heard on the foyer stairs, and so Kelly went downstairs later than Steven did. The sequence in which people left their 10 A.M. locations was therefore Cheryl, Taylor, Steven, Kelly, Brianna, Aria, Danny.

Taylor intended to slip out of 2A, murder the victim, and return to 2A before anyone noticed, but Charlotte was in the upstairs hall. So Taylor went downstairs, noted that the lounge was empty, and went back up the stairs as soon as Charlotte walked away. Taylor then committed the murder and went back down to the lounge, pretending to have been there ever since leaving guest room 2A.

Puzzle 4.1: Weighted Voting

Bestworld had 3 chips from Brianna, 2 chips each from Danny and
Steven, and 1 chip from Taylor, for a total of 8 chips.
Big Little Pies received 1 chip from Danny.
Boardwalk Umpire received 3 chips from Steven.
Breaking Bald received 3 chips from Kelly and 1 chip from Cheryl
for a total of 4 chips.
Counterparty received 1 chip from Steven.
Game of Clones received 3 chips each from Cheryl and Danny and
2 chips each from Brianna and Taylor for a total of 10 chips.
Masters of Hex received 3 chips from Aria and 2 chips from Kelly
for a total of 5 chips.
Outlandish received 3 chips from Taylor and 2 chips each from
Aria and Cheryl for a total of 7 chips.
Truly Bloody received 1 chip from Kelly.
Twin Beaks received 1 chip each from Aria and Brianna for a total
of 2 chips.

The guests' point totals were as follows: Aria 14, Brianna 20,
Cheryl 21, Danny 19, Kelly 10, Steven 12, and Taylor 25.

Since each of the seven guests awarded 6 chips, the 10 shows' chip
totals add up to 42. Since three totals are 1's and the others are all
different with 10 being the highest (clues 1 and 2), the chip totals
must be 1, 1, 1, 2, 3, 4, 5, 10, and one of the two combinations
adding up to 15: 6 and 9, or 7 and 8. In either case, the three highest
chip totals add up to 25, which is Taylor's point total (clue 11).

Danny's point total is 19, including votes for *Bestworld* and
Game of Clones (clue 8). Per clue 7, Danny's other vote was for
Big Little Pies, which he gave one chip. *Big Little Pies* received no
other votes, so he earned 1 point from it, and the point totals for
Bestworld and *Game of Clones* added up to 18. They must therefore
have scored 8 and 10 in some order, and the other highest chip-
getter, *Outlandish* (clue 11), received 7 chips. Taylor voted for
Bestworld and *Game of Clones* in addition to *Outlandish* (clue 11).

Brianna's point total was at least 20, and Cheryl's was 1 point
more than Brianna's (clue 5). Cheryl's vote for *Outlandish* (clue 6)
earned her 7 points; she can only just reach 21 points if *Breaking
Bald* got 4 chips (the highest possible, per clue 12), and *Game of
Clones* got 10 chips (which means *Bestworld* received 8 chips).
Brianna's point total was 20, therefore, at most 3 of which came
from *Twin Beaks* (clue 3). Brianna needed point totals of 7 and 10
with 3 from *Twin Beaks*, or 8 and 10 with a 2 from *Twin Beaks*.
But since *Breaking Bald* received 4 chips and *Boardwalk Umpire*
received more chips than *Twin Beaks* (clue 12), *Twin Beaks* must
have received 2 chips (single chips from Aria and Brianna, per
clue 3), *Boardwalk Umpire* received 3, and *Truly Bloody* received 1.
Brianna's 18 remaining points came from voting for *Bestworld*
and *Game of Clones*. We know *Counterparty* received only 1 chip
(clue 7), so by elimination, *Masters of Hex* received 5 chips. Since,
Brianna, Cheryl, Danny, and Taylor all voted for *Game of Clones*,
no one else can have voted for it (clue 13).

Because everyone else's point totals are accounted for, the guests
with totals of 10, 12, and 14 (clue 14) are Aria, Kelly, and Steven,
in some combination. The guest with a point total of 10 could have
achieved it by voting for shows with chip totals of 1-1-8, 1-2-7, 1-4-
5, or 2-3-5. The guest with a point total of 12 could have achieved it
by voting for shows with chip totals of 1-3-8, 1-4-7, 2-3-7, or 3-4-5.
The guest with a point total of 14 could have achieved it by voting
for shows with chip totals of 1-5-8, 2-4-8, 2-5-7, or 3-4-7 (1-3-10 is

not possible, since all the *Game of Clones* chips are accounted for).

Steven is known to have voted for *Counterparty*, which received
1 chip (clue 7), and *Boardwalk Umpire*, which received 3 (clue 10).
The only combination adding up to 10, 12, or 14 that includes both
a 1 and a 3 is 1-3-8, and so Steven's point total was 12 and his other
vote was for *Bestworld*.

Masters of Hex received 5 chips, and only two people remain
who could have voted for it (Aria and Kelly), and therefore both of
them did so. Kelly is also known to have voted for *Breaking Bald*,
which received 4 chips (clue 9). The only combination adding up to
10 or 14 that includes both a 4 and a 5 is 1-4-5, and so Kelly's point
total was 10 and her other vote was for *Truly Bloody* (the 1-chip
show not accounted for by another guest).

Aria therefore had a point total of 14. Since she is known to
have voted for *Twin Beaks* (clue 3) and *Masters of Hex*, her other
vote was for *Outlandish* (which received 7 chips).

Only Cheryl and Kelly voted for *Breaking Bald*, and they each
gave the show a different amount of chips (clue 9), so they gave 3
and 1 chips, in some order. We know Cheryl gave 3 chips to *Game
of Clones* and Kelly gave 1 chip to *Truly Bloody*, so Cheryl gave 1
chip to *Breaking Bald* and Kelly gave it 3 chips. By elimination,
Cheryl gave *Outlandish* 2 chips, and Kelly gave *Masters of Hex* 2
chips. Aria must have provided the rest of *Masters of Hex*'s 5 chips,
so she gave it 3 chips, and by elimination she gave *Outlandish* 2
chips. Aria and Cheryl's votes account for 4 of *Outlandish*'s 7 chips,
so Taylor gave it the other 3 chips.

Since no show received a set of three chips from more than two
guests (clue 15), *Game of Clones*'s chip total of 10 must have come
from two sets of 3 chips and two pairs of chips. Taylor, therefore,
gave *Game of Clones* 2 chips and gave *Bestworld* 1 chip. Brianna
and Taylor gave the same number of chips to one show (clue 4). It
can't be *Bestworld*, since Brianna gave 1 chip to *Twin Beaks*, so she
also gave 2 chips to *Game of Clones*. The chips corresponding to the
remaining votes can all be determined by elimination.

Puzzle 4.2: Murder in the Guest Wing

Brianna is the killer.

Aria's statement that all the other guests' statements are true
must be true, since if it were false, both she and at least one other
guest would be making false statements, contradicting Gordon's
statement that there is only one killer.

From clue 5, the haberdasher, illusionist, and locksmith are
in rooms 1A, 1B, and 2C, in some combination. From clue 11,
Aria, Brianna, and Kelly are in rooms 2A, 2B, and 2C, in some
combination. And from clue 12, Aria, Danny, and Kelly are the
judge, marketer, and neurologist, in some combination.

Brianna can only be in 2C, since 2A and 2B do not go with any
of her possible occupations; similarly, Danny can only be in 1C,
since his possible occupations can't be in 1A or 1B.

Steven and Taylor are in 1A and 1B in some combination,
and Aria and Kelly are in 2A and 2B in some combination. Since
Danny in 1C is not the illusionist or locksmith, clue 6 requires
Brianna in 2C to be either the illusionist or locksmith (since one of
the three in clue 6 must be in 1C or 2C). Brianna is therefore not
the haberdasher, and the haberdasher is in 1A or 1B.

Since Brianna and the judge have different room letters
(clue 10), Danny is not the judge. Since the judge's room letter
is different from Steven's (clue 13), the judge's must be the same
as Taylor's. Since Taylor and Kelly have different room letters
(clue 14), Aria's room letter must match Taylor's, and Aria must be
the judge. Since the judge is not in 1C and neither is the marketer

(per clue 8), Danny in 1C must be the neurologist. By elimination, then, since the marketer is not in 2A (clue 5), Aria the judge is in 2A, and Kelly is the marketer and is in room 2B.

Brianna in 2C can't be the illusionist (per clue 7, since the neurologist is in 1C), so she's the locksmith. Taylor isn't the illusionist (clue 6) so Taylor is the haberdasher and Steven is the illusionist. The letter of Steven's room is different from the judge's (clue 13), so Steven isn't in 1A; he's in 1B and Taylor is in 1A.

Clue 8 rules out the occupants of 1B, 1C, and 2B as being guilty, leaving 2C as the one room adjacent to the crawlspace that must have been occupied by the killer (clue 1).

Puzzle 4.3: 1830

In the morning game, Nolan came in first, Taylor came in second, Danny came in third, and Aria came in fourth. In the afternoon game, Cheryl came in first, Kelly came in second, Brianna came in third, and Steven came in fourth.

Aria owned C&O and CPR.
Brianna owned CPR and NYC.
Cheryl owned B&M and PRR.
Danny owned B&M and PRR.
Kelly owned B&O and NYNH.
Nolan owned NYC and NYNH.
Steven owned C&O and Erie.
Taylor owned B&O and Erie.

From clue 2, Aria and Taylor were two of the morning players. From clue 8, Steven played in the afternoon, and from clue 5 so did Cheryl. The PRR owner finished first or second in Kelly's game (clue 3), so Kelly and Nolan played in different games (clue 7). Brianna played in a different game from Nolan (clue 6), so she was in the same game as Kelly, and by elimination Danny was in the same game as Nolan.

From clue 2, neither Aria nor Taylor owned the PRR, nor did Kelly (clue 3). None of these three players therefore owned B&M (clue 9), nor did Brianna (clue 16), who therefore also did not own PRR. Since Cheryl and Steven played in the afternoon, the player who owned B&M in the morning was either Danny or Nolan. Therefore, Danny and Nolan played in the morning, and Brianna and Kelly played in the afternoon.

From clue 2, Taylor finished first or second. From clue 7, the PRR owner finished third in the morning game, so Aria finished fourth (clue 2), which means she owned C&O (clue 10).

From clue 3, the PRR owner in the afternoon finished first or second, Kelly finished second or third, and the NYC owner finished third or fourth. But since NYC did not finish fourth (clue 13), NYC finished third, Kelly finished second, and the PRR owner finished first.

From clues 4 and 14, the Erie owner in the morning finished second, Danny finished third (and so owned PRR), and the CPR owner finished fourth (and is therefore Aria).

From clue 5, Cheryl finished first or second, the B&O owner finished second or third, Steven finished third or fourth, and neither Cheryl nor Steven owned B&O. Since we already know Kelly finished second, however, Cheryl finished first and owned PRR. She and the other PRR owner, Danny, also owned B&M (clue 9).

From clue 12, the NYNH cannot have been owned by Brianna or Steven, neither of whom finished higher than third in the afternoon game, and since Cheryl's public companies are both accounted for, Kelly owned NYNH.

Taylor did not own NYC (clue 15) or C&O or CPR (Aria owned

both), so the company that both Steven and Taylor owned (per clue 8) was Erie. Taylor, therefore, finished second (it's already been established that the Erie's owner finished second in the morning game) and Nolan was first. Brianna was therefore third (clue 6) and owned NYC, and Steven was fourth and owned C&O (clue 10).

In the morning game, the B&O owner finished first or second, and in the afternoon game, the B&O owner finished second or third. They therefore must both have finished second, per clue 11, so Taylor and Kelly were the owners of B&O.

By elimination, Brianna owned CPR, and Nolan owned NYC and NYNH.

Puzzle 4.4: 1856

Taylor finished first, bought the Waterloo & Saugeen Railway Co. and Great Lakes Shipping Company, and owned the CV, GT, and TGB railroads.
Cheryl finished second, bought Flos Tramway and the Canada Company, and owned the GW, LPS, and WGB railroads.
Nolan finished third, bought the Niagara Falls Suspension Bridge Company, and owned the BBG, THB, and WR railroads.
Kelly finished fourth, bought the St. Clair Frontier Tunnel Company, and owned the CA and CPR railroads.

From clues 1 and 2, all 11 public companies were owned. One player owned CA and CPR, one owned BBG, THB, and WR, and two players each owned three of the other six companies.

From clues 3 and 4, one player owned LPS, WGB, and either CV or GW. By elimination, another player owned GT, TGB, and either CV or GW. Since GT and GW were owned by different players (clue 6), one player owned CV, GT, and TGB and another owned GW, LPS, and WGB.

From clues 6 and 7, the owner of CV, GT, and TGB finished ahead of the owner of GW, LPS, and WGB (who also bought the Canada Company, per clue 4), who finished ahead of the owner of BBG, THB, and WR. The first two of these three sets of companies were owned by Taylor and the buyer of the Flos Tramway (clue 3), in some order.

The buyer of the Niagara Falls Suspension Bridge Company finished third or fourth (clue 5), and Cheryl finished one place better (clue 8). Since Cheryl did not finish third (clue 1), she finished second and therefore the Niagara Falls Suspension Bridge buyer finished third.

Cheryl did not own CA and CPR (clue 1). If Cheryl owned CV, GT, and TGB, then Taylor owned GW, LPS, and WGB and finished third, and the owner of BBG, THB, and WR finished fourth. But Kelly did not finish first or own these last three companies (clue 2), so Cheryl must have owned GW, LPS, and WGB. Taylor owned CV, GT, and TGB and finished first. By elimination, Kelly owned CA and CPR, and didn't finish third (clue 1), so she finished fourth. Nolan, then, owned BBG, THB, and WR, and finished third, so he's the buyer of the Niagara Falls Suspension Bridge. Kelly bought the St. Clair Frontier Tunnel Company (clue 5).

Cheryl bought the Flos Tramway (per clue 3, since Taylor owned CV) as well as the Canada Company (per clue 4, since she owned LPS and WGB). Taylor bought the Great Lakes Shipping Company (per clue 1), and therefore also bought Waterloo & Saugeen Railway Co. (clue 9).

Weekend 5

Puzzle 5.1: Major Arcana

Aria: 8, 11, 15 (total of 34)
Brianna: 1, 12, 18 (total of 31)
Cheryl: 5, 14, 16 (total of 35)
Danny: 6, 7, 20 (total of 33)
Kelly: 4, 10, 13 (total of 27)
Steven: 2, 9, 21 (total of 32)
Taylor: 3, 17, 19 (total of 39)

From clues 1, 2, and 3, Brianna has a square and two leftovers.

The sum of the numbers on all the cards is 231. From clue 4, the sum of the five totals for the guests other than Kelly and Taylor is (Brianna's score × 5) + 10.

Since Steven has no leftovers (clue 1), his high card is either 19 or 21 (clue 5). Since his square is odd, there are only a few ways he can have an even number: if he has the 2, his cards are 1-2-21 or 2-9-21; if he does not, his cards are 1-6-19, 1-10-19, or 1-14-19. That gives him possible card totals of 24, 32, 26, 30, or 34. Steven's score is one greater than Brianna's, so the possible total scores of the five guests besides Kelly and Taylor (using the formula above) are 125, 165, 135, 155, and 175.

Let's look now at Taylor and Kelly's scores. Kelly's prime is one less than the sum of her other two cards (clue 6). Of all the possible sums of the squares and prime products (per the makeup of her hand from clue 1), only two are one greater than one of the prime cards (4 + 10 and 4 + 14). But, also per clue 6, her prime isn't 17, so her hand is 4-10-13, totaling 27. Taylor's highest-scoring possible hand, then, is 11-17-19 (since Kelly has the 13), scoring 47, for a maximum Kelly + Taylor total of 74. The difference between 231 and 74 is 157, which means the five other players must score at least that much between them, eliminating all possibilities for Steven except 2-9-21 and 1-14-19. If Steven's hand is 1-14-19, totaling 34, then Brianna's would total 33 (clue 4). Brianna, as previously noted, has two leftovers and a square; all the leftovers are even, so for a total of 33 her square must be odd. The 1 is part of Steven's 1-14-19 hand, so that leaves only the 9, with a remainder of 24 for the two leftovers. No combination of two leftovers adds up to 24, so this is impossible, and Steven must have 2-9-21, scoring 32. Aria's total is 34, Brianna's 31, Cheryl's 35, and Danny's 33. We know Kelly's hand totals 27, so Taylor's totals 39.

Brianna holds one square (of which Kelly has the 4 and Steven has the 9) and two leftovers, which all together total 31. All the leftovers are even, so her square must be odd, so she has the 1 (the only remaining odd square), and her two leftovers total 30, so they are 12 and 18. By elimination, Cheryl's square is the 16. Her other cards add up to 19 and must be 5 and 14 (they can't be 6 and 13, because Kelly has the 13). The remaining primes that Taylor could hold are the 3, 7, 11, 17, and 19, which total 57. Since 57 − 39 = 18, the two cards Taylor doesn't hold must total 18. Those can only be 7 and 11, so Taylor's hand is 3-17-19.

Aria's leftover can't be the 20, since there's no way to get a sum of 14 from her other two cards, so she holds the 8, and her other cards total 26 and must be the 11 and 15. By elimination, Danny's hand is 6-7-20.

Puzzle 5.2: Birdhouses

Birdhouses are located on Duck Island and near the boathouse, the lighthouse, the mansion, the pond, and the windmill.

Statements 2 and 5 cannot both be true, since they are contradictory about whether the cottage is a birdhouse site. Statements 3 and 4 also cannot both be true, since they are contradictory about whether the bridge is a birdhouse site. Since there is only one false statement in each set, only one of the statements 2 and 3 is false, and only one of the statements 4 and 5 is false. It also follows that statements 1 and 6 are true, and there are birdhouses near the boathouse, lighthouse, and mansion, and on Duck Island.

It also follows that only one of the statements 2 and 5 is false; for if they were both false, both statements 3 and 4 would have to be true, which is not the case. Similarly, only one of the statements 3 and 4 can be false.

Since one of the statements 2 and 5 is true, there is a birdhouse near the windmill; and since one of the statements 3 and 4 is true, there is a birdhouse near the pond. (The false statements are 2 and 4.)

Puzzle 5.3: Wildflowers

Brianna, Cheryl, Kelly, and Taylor visited the boathouse, which has two kinds of wildflowers: prickly-pear cactus and windflower.
Aria, Brianna, Danny, Kelly, and Steven visited the bridge, which has two kinds of wildflowers: Canada violet and yellow passionflower.
Aria, Danny, and Kelly visited the cottage, which has three kinds of wildflowers: acony bell, fire pink, and little sweet Betsy.
Brianna, Kelly, Steven, and Taylor visited Duck Island, which has only trailing bluet.
Brianna and Kelly visited the lighthouse, which has only atamasco lily.
Cheryl, Danny, and Taylor visited Lookout Point, which has three kinds of wildflowers: Carolina jasmine, common toadflax, and crane-fly orchid.
Aria, Danny, and Taylor visited the pond, which has three kinds of wildflowers: heliotrope, jack-in-the-pulpit, and trillium.
Aria, Cheryl, and Steven visited the old hut, which has two kinds of wildflowers: bloodroot and coral honeysuckle.
Aria, Cheryl, Danny, Steven, and Taylor visited the old well, which has two kinds of wildflowers: cardinal flower and spiderwort.
Brianna, Cheryl, and Steven visited the windmill, which has only mayapple.

Danny brought back 13 kinds of wildflowers, Aria 12, Taylor 11, Cheryl 10, Kelly 9, Steven 8, and Brianna 7.

From clues 1 and 2: The fewest wildflower varieties a guest could bring back was 7 (if the guest visited the three one-wildflower locations and two locations with two), and the most was 13 (the three three-wildflower locations and two locations with two). Since no two guests brought back the same number of wildflower varieties (clue 2), they must have brought back every possible number of wildflowers from 7 through 13, and the total number of wildflowers found was 70.

From clue 7, the locations with one wildflower are Duck Island, the lighthouse, and the windmill. From clues 1 and 14 and the fact that the boathouse had at least two kinds of wildflowers, the locations with three wildflower varieties are the cottage, Lookout Point, and the pond. The other locations each have two kinds of wildflowers.

Clues 5 and 6 identify the two locations (bridge and old well) visited by five guests, and the identities of those guests. Clues 8, 9, and 11 identify three locations (pond, cottage, and windmill) that were visited by three guests, and clue 10 identifies the old hut as a fourth (visited by Aria, Cheryl, and Steven, per clue 6).

Danny went to the bridge (clue 5), the old well (clue 6), and the cottage (clue 9) but not the old hut (clue 10), boathouse (clue 12), or any of Duck Island, the lighthouse, or the windmill (clue 7). By elimination, Danny went to Lookout Point and the pond. Since Brianna's only location shared with Danny is the bridge (clue 12), she did not visit the cottage, Lookout Point, or the pond, nor the old well or old hut (clues 6 and 10). She visited the boathouse, Duck Island, the lighthouse, and the windmill (in addition to the bridge). Brianna visited locations having a total of 7 varieties of wildflowers, and Danny visited locations with 13.

Since Aria and Brianna both went to the bridge (clue 5), they shared no other location (clue 13). Aria therefore did not go to the boathouse, Duck Island, lighthouse, or windmill, but did go to the pond, old hut, and old well (clues 6, 8, and 10). Whether her remaining location was the cottage or Lookout Point, her total number of wildflower varieties was 12.

From clues 7 and 15, since mayapple but not prickly-pear cactus is located at Duck Island, the lighthouse, or the windmill, and since Cheryl did not go to the bridge, prickly-pear cactus is located at the boathouse (along with windflower, per clue 8), and Cheryl went there. Cheryl went to the windmill as well (clue 11). Per clue 15, since Brianna and Cheryl's two locations in common were the boathouse and windmill, Cheryl did not go to Duck Island or the lighthouse, and mayapple is at the windmill. Since Steven did not visit the lighthouse (clue 16), he brought back trailing bluet from Duck Island, and atamasco lily is located at the lighthouse (clue 7). Steven's other four locations are known to be the bridge, old hut, old well, and windmill (clues 5, 6, 10, and 11), and he brought back 8 varieties of wildflowers.

Kelly visited the cottage (clue 9), and we know Aria visited the pond, so the location where Cheryl, Danny, and Taylor found both Carolina jasmine and common toadflax (clue 17) cannot be the cottage or the pond, either of which would then have had more than three guests visiting, and so must be Lookout Point (where crane-fly orchid is also found, per clue 8). Cheryl visited locations with a total of 10 kinds of wildflowers.

To account for the boathouse's four guests (clue 14), both Kelly and Taylor visited it. Neither of them visited the windmill, whose three guests are accounted for.

Since Brianna and Kelly visited four locations in common (clue 13), Kelly went to Duck Island and the lighthouse, for a total of 9 kinds of wildflowers. By elimination, Taylor was the third guest at the pond. To reach a total of 11 wildflowers, the only number not accounted for by another guest, Taylor's remaining location (besides the boathouse, Lookout Point, pond, and old well) had to have just one wildflower, and so was either Duck Island or the lighthouse. Aria is therefore the third guest who went to the cottage. Since only the lighthouse can be the two-guest location mentioned in clue 3, Taylor went to Duck Island.

The Canada violet referred to in clue 11 must have been at the bridge (found along with yellow passionflower, per clue 5), since all the wildflowers are accounted for at the other locations visited by Brianna and by Cheryl or Steven but not both. Since little sweet Betsy and fire pink were found at the cottage (clue 9), the only three-wildflower location with two open spots for jack-in-the-pulpit and trillium (clue 18) is the pond (to go with heliotrope,

per clue 8). Spiderwort was found by the old well (clue 6), so by elimination, bloodroot and coral honeysuckle are located at the old hut (clue 19). Cardinal flower is at the old well (not the cottage, which Taylor—who found cardinal flower per clue 20—did not visit), and acony bell is growing at the cottage.

Puzzle 5.4: Murder at the Lighthouse

Danny is the killer. His whereabouts between 12:30 and 1:30 cannot be determined, but every other guest can be placed in a particular room of the mansion from 12 to 1:30.

Aria, the rancher, was in the lounge from 12 to 12:30 and the dining room from 12:30 to 1:30.

Brianna, the teacher, was in the small game room from 12 to 1 and the dining room from 1 to 1:30.

Cheryl, the oceanographer, was in the small game room from 12 to 1 and the dining room from 1 to 1:30.

Danny, the speculator, was in the dining room from 12 to 12:30 and then left the mansion to commit the murder.

Kelly, the undertaker, was in the lounge from 12 to 12:30, the dining room from 12:30 to 1, and the small game room from 1 to 1:30.

Steven, the quizmaster, was in the dining room from 12 to 12:30 and the small game room from 12:30 to 1:30.

Taylor, the promoter, was in the lounge from 12 to 12:30, the dining room from 12:30 to 1, and the small game room from 1 to 1:30.

From Aria's, Brianna's, and Danny's statements, as well as Evelyn's statement about the time guests spent in the dining room, the following sets of guests were in the dining room during the three half-hour periods, in some order: Aria, the promoter, and the undertaker; Brianna, the oceanographer, and the rancher; and Danny and the quizmaster. One guest—and only one guest, since every guest spent at least a half-hour in the dining room (clue 5)—must be in two of these groups.

From clue 13, Kelly and the promoter were in the same room each period, and so from clue 9, Kelly is the undertaker.

Since Danny spent only half an hour in the dining room (clue 5), he was not in one of the dining room groups of three and is not the oceanographer, promoter, or rancher; we know he isn't the quizmaster (clue 12), nor can he be the teacher unless Cheryl were the quizmaster (clue 11), which she is not (clue 6). By elimination, Danny is the speculator.

If Taylor was with just one other guest in the dining room, Taylor is the quizmaster. If Taylor was with two other guests in the dining room, Taylor is the promoter (not the rancher, who is in the same group with the oceanographer, with whom Taylor never shared a room, per clue 15).

In each half-hour time period, seven guests will have occupied the three rooms in some combination, except that one guest must have been gone for two consecutive half-hour periods to have committed the crime. Taylor was either in three rooms with one other guest each or three rooms with two other guests each (clue 15). But consider that there are two dining room periods with three guests (clues 9 and 10) and two small game room periods with three guests (clue 6). At least two of those periods must have happened during the same 30-minute time period. If Taylor occupied one of the rooms each period with just one other guest, then there would have to be one period with three guests in the dining room, three guests in the small game room, and two guests in the lounge. That's eight people, but there are only seven guests, so this is impossible.

Therefore Taylor was in three rooms with two other guests each and is the promoter, and Kelly and one other guest were in the lounge and small game room with Taylor in different half-hour periods (clue 13). Since Cheryl was not the quizmaster (clue 6), she was in the dining room group of Brianna, the oceanographer, and the rancher, which means that Brianna is the teacher (clue 11). Because Cheryl spent the first two half-hours in the small game room (clue 6), Brianna did too (clue 11), and they both had to be in the dining room from 1 to 1:30. Since Danny preceded the undertaker in the dining room (clue 5), Danny was there from 12 to 12:30 and the group of Aria, Kelly, and Taylor were there from 12:30 to 1. Kelly and Taylor were always in the same room (clue 13) and Taylor was in three different rooms (clue 15). They weren't in the small game room from 12 to 12:30 since Brianna and Cheryl were there, and that's too many people (clue 15), so they were in the small game room from 1 to 1:30 and the lounge from 12 to 12:30.

Steven spent two consecutive periods in the small game room (clue 14), so he had to be there from 12:30 to 1. If he was also there from 12 to 12:30 with Brianna and Cheryl, then that would leave only Aria unaccounted for during that period, and since she could not be both the third person in the lounge and Danny's companion in the dining room, this is impossible. Steven, therefore, was in the small game room from 1 to 1:30.

By now it is clear that only Danny had an opportunity to commit the crime, and so he was absent from the mansion from 12:30 to 1:30. Aria, by elimination, was in the dining room with Brianna and Cheryl from 1 to 1:30, and is either the rancher or oceanographer. But since she shared a room with Taylor, she can't be the oceanographer, so she's the rancher and Cheryl is the oceanographer. By elimination, Steven is the quizmaster and so was in the dining room with Danny from 12 to 12:30 (clue 12), and Aria was the third person in the lounge during that time with Kelly and Taylor.

Weekend 6

Puzzle 6.1: Amusement Park

Aria, whose favorite ride was the carousel, won an alligator by
    playing coin toss.
Brianna, whose favorite ride was the drop tower, won a zebra by
    playing Skee-Ball.
Cheryl, whose favorite ride was the roller coaster, won a panda by
    playing balloon and dart.
Danny, whose favorite ride was the pirate ship, won a dog by
    playing high striker.
Kelly, whose favorite ride was the Tilt-A-Whirl, won a tiger by
    playing basketball.
Steven, whose favorite ride was bumper boats, won a lion by
    playing milk bottle.
Taylor, whose favorite ride was the Ferris wheel, won a whale by
    playing water gun.

From clue 4, the favorite rides of Aria, Cheryl, Kelly, and Steven were bumper boats, carousel, roller coaster, and Tilt-A-Whirl, in some combination. From clue 5, the dog, lion, tiger, and whale were won by playing basketball, high striker, milk bottle, and water gun, in some combination. From clue 6, the guests whose favorite rides were bumper boats, carousel, drop tower, and Ferris wheel won prizes at coin toss, milk bottle, Skee-Ball, and water gun, in some combination. From clue 7, Aria, Brianna, Kelly, and Taylor won an alligator, a tiger, a whale, and a zebra, in some combination. From clue 8, the guests whose favorite rides were carousel, drop

tower, Ferris wheel, and pirate ship won an alligator, a dog, a whale, and a zebra, in some combination. From clue 9, Aria, Brianna, Cheryl, and Danny won prizes at balloon and dart, coin toss, high striker, and Skee-Ball, in some combination.

From clues 4 and 8, Danny had no possible favorite ride that the lion or panda winner could have had, and by elimination he won a plush dog. Cheryl and Steven are the only guests who could have won the lion and panda, and so they did in some combination, and the carousel was not the favorite ride of either (clue 8). From clue 5, Danny did not win the dog by playing balloon and dart, coin toss, or Skee-Ball, and by elimination won at high striker. The only possible favorite ride for Danny mentioned in clue 4 that could be the favorite ride of the high striker winner as mentioned in clue 6 is the pirate ship, which was therefore Danny's favorite ride.

Brianna and Taylor must have drop tower and Ferris wheel as their favorite rides in some combination, and so neither won a prize at balloon and dart or basketball (clue 6), and neither won a tiger (clue 8).

Aria played balloon and dart, coin toss, or Skee-Ball, and so did not win a tiger or whale (clue 5). Brianna played coin toss or Skee-Ball and so did not win a whale. By elimination, Kelly won the tiger and was therefore not the person whose favorite ride was the carousel (clue 8). Aria and Brianna can only have won the alligator and zebra, and so they did in some combination, which means that Taylor won the whale.

By elimination, Aria's favorite ride was the carousel, and so she did not win at balloon and dart (clue 6). By elimination, Cheryl played balloon and dart, which means that her favorite ride was not bumper boats (clue 6) and that her prize was the panda (since from clue 5 the other choices for the balloon and dart player were the alligator and zebra, which Aria and Brianna won in some combination). By elimination, Steven won the lion.

From clue 10, the alligator was won by the coin toss player, the zebra was won by the Skee-Ball player, and Brianna's favorite ride was not the Ferris wheel. By elimination, Taylor's favorite ride was the Ferris wheel and Brianna's was the drop tower.

From clue 11, Kelly's favorite ride was not bumper boats, Kelly did not play water gun, and the guest whose favorite ride was bumper boats did not play water gun. By elimination, Steven's favorite ride was bumper boats, which means that Steven did not play basketball (clue 6). By elimination, Kelly won at basketball, Steven at milk bottle, and Taylor at water gun.

From clue 12, the Tilt-A-Whirl fan won a tiger and was Kelly, so Cheryl's favorite ride was the roller coaster. Aria won the alligator at coin toss, and Brianna won the zebra at Skee-Ball.

Puzzle 6.2: Miniature Golf

The completed scorecard for all the players is shown at the top of the next page.

From clue 12, Danny birdied the 13th hole (as did Aria and Brianna), and so Danny's 10 consecutive pars (clue 5) had to include the 3rd through 10th holes. That includes a 3 on the 8th hole, which means that everyone's scores on the 8th hole were 3's (clue 10). Danny's four consecutive 3's (clue 2) had to include holes 15 through 17.

From clue 13, Aria, Brianna, and Cheryl had 2's on the 2nd and 3rd holes. Danny must have had a 3 on the 2nd hole—not a 1 on account of clue 12, and not more than 3 because of clue 1. Danny's streak of pars therefore included the 11th and 12th holes, and the scores on the 16th hole were a 3 by Danny and three 2's (clue 14).

Cheryl's six consecutive bogeys (clue 4) must have included the 10th through 14th holes. Aria's eight consecutive 3's (clue 2) must have included holes 5 through 11. Brianna's five consecutive birdies (clue 3) had to include holes 11 through 13. (She can't have birdied holes 3 through 7, since birdies on holes 4 and 7 would contradict clue 12.) Aria's four consecutive birdies (clue 3) had to be on holes 12 through 15, and so Aria had a 3 on the 4th hole to complete her streak of 3's.

From clue 7, two players had identical scores for the first four holes, and neither of these was Danny, who did not match the others' scores on the 2nd and 3rd holes. Danny is therefore part of the pair who had the same scores on holes 4 through 9. The other member of that pair cannot be Aria, whose scores don't match Danny's on several holes. Nor can it be Brianna, whose four consecutive bogeys (clue 4) must have been on holes 4 through 7. Cheryl therefore had pars on holes 4 through 9, so her run of consecutive bogeys included the 15th hole. From clue 12, she had a 1 on the first hole.

Brianna's score on the 10th hole was not a 1 (clue 16) or 2 (clue 11), and so was a 3. Her five birdies were therefore on holes 11 through 15, and she must have had one more hole-in-one (from clue 9 and the fact that Aria had 1's on the 13th and 14th holes). That 1 can only be on a hole with par 2, but not the first hole (clue 12), so it was the 17th hole. Also per clue 9, Cheryl had more 1's than Danny, and her other 1 must also be on the 17th hole.

From clue 8, Aria had a 2 on the 17th hole and Danny had 2's on both the 1st and 14th holes. Danny's run of four 3's (clue 2) therefore includes the 18th hole, so everyone scored 3 on that hole (clue 10). Each set of holes had one player who posted the lowest score, and each round's lowest-scoring player was different (clue 6). Brianna had the lowest score in the final third, so she did not have the lowest score in the middle third. Danny's score of 16 in the middle third must have been the winning score, so Brianna can't have scored less than 17 on that set of holes, and therefore scored 4 on the 9th hole.

Brianna had more 2's than Cheryl (clue 15), so Brianna must have scored 2 on the first hole, as did Aria (clue 7), the overall winner of the game.

	Par	Aria	Brianna	Cheryl	Danny
1. The L	2	2	2	1	2
2. The T	2	2	2	2	3
3. The U	3	2	2	2	3
4. The Y	2	3	3	2	2
5. The Z	3	3	4	3	3
6. The W	4	3	5	4	4
First Third Total	16	15	18	14	17
7. The Tunnel	2	3	3	2	2
8. The Bridge	3	3	3	3	3
9. The Castle	3	3	4	3	3
10. The Ramp	2	3	3	3	2
11. The Loop	3	3	2	4	3
12. The Windmill	3	2	2	4	3
Middle Third Total	16	17	17	19	16
13. The Cave	2	1	1	3	1
14. The Plateau	2	1	1	3	2
15. The Cliffs	4	3	3	5	3
16. The Waterfall	2	2	2	2	3
17. The Lake	2	2	1	1	3
18. The Hills	4	3	3	3	3
Final Third Total	16	12	11	17	15
Total Score	48	44	46	50	48

Puzzle 6.3: Hard Candy

Aria bought peppermint hard candy at the Olde Candy Shoppe and shared it with Cheryl.

Brianna bought butterscotch hard candy at Guilty Pleasures and shared it with Danny.

Cheryl bought strawberry hard candy at Sweet Dreams and shared it with Kelly.

Danny bought apple hard candy at the Olde Candy Shoppe and shared it with Steven.

Kelly bought orange hard candy at the Olde Candy Shoppe and shared it with Taylor.

Steven bought raspberry hard candy at Sweet Dreams and shared it with Brianna.

Taylor bought cinnamon hard candy at Guilty Pleasures and shared it with Aria.

From clue 1, Brianna, Danny, Kelly, and Taylor bought apple, butterscotch, orange, and raspberry candy, in some combination. From clue 2, the butterscotch, orange, peppermint, and raspberry candy were shared with Brianna, Cheryl, Danny, and Taylor, in some combination.

Clues 3, 4, and 5 indicate where the candy shared with five of the guests was bought, and clue 6 rules out Aria and Danny as shoppers at Guilty Pleasure, rules out Steven and Taylor as shoppers at the Olde Candy Shoppe, and rules out Kelly as a shopper at Sweet Dreams. From clue 9, Cheryl didn't shop at the Olde Candy Shoppe either.

From clues 3, 4, and 5, one store had to be patronized by three guests and the other two stores by two guests each. Since Guilty Pleasures was one of the stores where just two guests bought candy, the guests who bought orange and peppermint (clue 10) did not shop there.

Aria shared candy with Cheryl (clue 12), so Aria must have bought peppermint candy. Cheryl, then, bought either cinnamon or strawberry candy, neither of which was shared with Taylor, so she didn't share with Taylor, and neither did Brianna, Danny, or Steven (clue 11), so Kelly shared her candy with Taylor and therefore she shopped at the Olde Candy Shoppe (clue 4).

The butterscotch candy was shared with Danny (clue 13) and so must have been bought at Guilty Pleasures (clue 3), where the cinnamon candy was also bought (clue 7), and since only two people shopped there, no other candy was bought there. The cinnamon candy was shared with Aria (clue 3). The strawberry candy was bought by either Cheryl or Taylor, neither of whom shopped at the Olde Candy Shoppe, so it was bought at Sweet Dreams, as was the raspberry candy (clue 8). Since no more than three candies were ever bought in the same store, the orange and peppermint candies were bought at the Olde Candy Shoppe, and Danny shopped there as well (clue 10). By elimination, he bought apple candy. Since Aria bought the peppermint candy from the Olde Candy Shoppe, Kelly also shopped there, so the candy she shared with Taylor was orange.

Danny's apple candy wasn't shared with Brianna (clue 2), so Danny shared it with Steven (clue 11). Brianna, then, must be the person who shared the butterscotch candy bought at Guilty Pleasures with Danny, and Steven shared candy (which, by elimination, was raspberry) with Brianna (clue 11). Steven bought the raspberry candy at Sweet Dreams, so Cheryl is the person who bought strawberry candy there (clue 9). By elimination, Taylor bought the cinnamon candy from Guilty Pleasures, and is the one who shared it with Aria, and Cheryl shared her strawberry candy from Sweet Dreams with Kelly.

Weekend 7

Puzzle 7.1: Fantasy Chess Draft

Aria drafted, in order: 2 B+N, 2 R+F, 2 F, 1 W.
Cheryl drafted, in order: 2 B+W, 2 N+C, 2 F+W, 1 F.
Danny drafted, in order: 2 R+B, 2 N, 2 B, 1 F.
Gordon drafted, in order: 1 R+B, 2 N+F, 2 N+W, 2 W.
Steven drafted, in order: 1 R+N, 2 R, 2 C+F, 2 W.
Taylor drafted, in order: 2 R, 2 B, 2 N, 1 R+N.

Since each of the six players drafted seven pieces, there were exactly 21 combo pieces drafted (clue 7). No one can have drafted zero combo pieces, because the most they could then have spent would have been 16 points (for example, pairs of R, B, and N basic pieces and a single basic C piece would only cost 16 points), contrary to clue 2. Nor can anyone have drafted seven combo pieces, since even if the others drafted one, two, three, four, and five combo pieces, the total of 22 would be one more than 21. From clue 8, Taylor drafted exactly one combo piece and the other players drafted two, three, four, five, and six combo pieces, in some combination.

Per clue 4, 10 pieces were drafted in the first round, so three of the pieces mentioned in clue 6 must be R+B pieces, making the sequence of pieces in that round 4 B pieces, 3 R+B pieces, and 3 R pieces. Since the single-piece drafts were consecutive, the first round consisted of two pairs of B pieces followed by a pair of R+B pieces and a single R+B piece, followed by a single R piece and a pair of R pieces. Aria, Cheryl, Danny, and Taylor's single pieces were all drafted in round 4 (clue 4).

Taylor's combo piece can only be the single piece drafted in the final round, which means that Taylor's first-round pick was a pair of basic R pieces for 6 points. To reach 19 points, Taylor must have drafted two basic pairs of B, N, or C pieces and drafted a 5-point piece in the final round, which could only be R+N or R+C, since the R+B pieces were all drafted in the first round.

Aria spent 8 points in each of the first two rounds (clue 3) and must have drafted pairs of combo pieces worth 4 in each. That only leaves three points available for her final three pieces, which are therefore basic F and W pieces, so she ended up with a total of four combo pieces. Steven's single R piece in the first round can't be a basic R piece, because another pair of basic R pieces was drafted at some other time, per clue 12. (They can't be the pair Taylor drafted because the following draft was a combo piece by Aria.) So Steven's single-piece draft was a combo piece. Since Gordon and Steven drafted only pairs of pieces after the first round, they are the only two besides Taylor who can have an odd number of combo pieces (one must have three and the other five). By elimination, Cheryl and Danny have two and six combo pieces, in some combination. Danny, however, spent 10 points in the first round on his pair of R+B pieces, and if he bought two more pairs of combo pieces, it would be impossible to spend less than 10 points on them (by buying the one pair of 2-point F+W pieces and one pair of any of the 3-point pieces), and he only has 9 points left to spend. He therefore has two combo pieces and Cheryl has six.

In the final three rounds Gordon drafted four N pieces and four W pieces (clue 9), which is only possible if a pair of N+W pieces is included. Since no W pieces were drafted in the second round (clue 10), and the only pairs of pieces drafted in the fourth round were two matching pairs of basic pieces (clues 4 and 15), Gordon drafted a pair of N+W pieces in the third round and a pair of basic W pieces in round four. Steven, the only other player to draft a pair of pieces in round 4, also drafted two basic W pieces, per clue 15. Gordon spent 5 points in round 1, 6 in round 3, and 2 in round 4,

leaving 6 points available in round two, which can only have been spent on a pair of N+F pieces, giving him five combo pieces. Steven therefore had three combo pieces.

Cheryl spent 8 points in round 2 (clue 3), leaving 11 points for her remaining 5 pieces. As we've shown, the smallest amount she could spend for two more pairs of combo pieces is 10, and that's what she must have spent, leaving her with one point to buy a basic F or W piece in round 4. Her pair of B combo pieces in round one must be B+W, since all other B combo pieces cost 4 or more, and her round 3 pair must be the 2-point combo piece F+W. Since her pieces collectively had five different types of movement (clue 14), and we've only accounted for three (B, F, and W, which is the case whichever piece she chose for her round 4 draft), her round 2 combo piece must be a 4-point piece using two movements that none of her other pieces use. The only such piece is N+C.

Per clue 5, the only C pieces drafted were two pairs, with eight other drafts between them. There aren't enough drafts before Cheryl's second-round draft of two N+C pieces to account for those eight, so the other pair of C pieces can only have been Steven's third-round draft. Since that accounts for all C pieces, Aria's round 1 pick must have been B+N, and Taylor's round 4 pick was R+N. Aria's round 2 draft pair was also a 4-point combo piece (and, again, not a C piece), so it was R+F.

The pair of basic R pieces drafted just before a pair of basic B pieces (clue 12) must have been Steven's second-round pick, which means that Taylor drafted two basic B pieces in the second round. The two pairs of basic N pieces drafted in different rounds (clue 13) must have been Danny's round 2 draft and Taylor's round 3 draft. All four basic B pieces were drafted (clue 11), and the second pair of basic B pieces can only have been drafted by Danny in the third round.

Steven spent 6 points in round 2 (on basic R pieces) and 2 points in round 4 (on basic W pieces), leaving him 11 points to spend on the rest of his pieces. The pair of pieces in round 3 will cost an even amount of points no matter what, so the single combo R piece he drafted in round 1 must cost an odd amount. All the R+B pieces are accounted for, R+C isn't an option because no other C pieces were drafted, and R+F only costs 4 points, so it was R+N, leaving 6 points to spend on round 3's combo C piece. Steven's pieces use five different types of movement (clue 14), and his other pieces collectively use R, N, and W, so round 3's draft can't be C+W and must be C+F.

Since all four basic F pieces were drafted (clue 11), Aria must have drafted a pair of them in the third round (requiring her to spend her last point on a basic W piece in the fourth round), and Cheryl and Danny each drafted a basic F piece in the fourth round.

Puzzle 7.2: Fantasy Chess Tournament

The final point totals were Taylor 4, Gordon 3.5, Aria 3, Cheryl 2.5, Danny 2, and Steven 0.

The strengths of the players' armies were ranked Danny 1, Aria 2, Taylor 3, Gordon 4, Steven 5, and Cheryl 6. (Details on the rankings of the pieces and armies can be found at the end of the answer to this puzzle.)

In consecutive rounds, players had the following results:

Aria lost to Taylor, won against Steven, drew with Gordon, won against Cheryl, and drew with Danny.
Cheryl won against Danny, drew with Gordon, lost to Taylor, lost to Aria, and won against Steven.

Danny lost to Cheryl, lost to Taylor, won against Steven, drew with Gordon, and drew with Aria.

Gordon won against Steven, drew with Cheryl, drew with Aria, drew with Danny, and won against Taylor.

Steven lost to Gordon, Aria, Danny, Taylor, and Cheryl.

Taylor won against Aria, Danny, Cheryl, and Steven before losing to Gordon.

Since the only undefeated player did not come in first (clue 1), the most points anyone had was 4. The three players whose point totals are 1 more than their army rank per clue 3 must therefore be the armies ranked 1, 2, and 3. Since two other players finished with 3.5 and 2.5 points, per clue 4, one player must have ended up with 0 points (since the sum of the other point totals is 15, the number of games played).

By elimination, Gordon played Steven in round 1 (clue 5). Because Cheryl and Taylor played White in round 1 (clue 5), neither of them has the top-ranked army (since whoever has the weaker army moves first), but one of their opponents (Danny and Aria) might. Since Aria and Taylor met in round 1 instead of round 5, they cannot have the top two armies in rank (clue 2), and they also can't have the top- and bottom-ranked armies, since Gordon played White more times than Taylor (clue 8) and thus has a weaker army. At best, Aria is ranked 2, Taylor is ranked 3, and Gordon is ranked 4. Since Gordon played White fewer times than Steven (clue 8), Gordon's army ranks above Steven's. By elimination, Danny's army must be ranked 1, and his first-round opponent Cheryl's army has a rank of 6. Aria's army's rank is 2, and the armies of Taylor, Gordon, and Steven are ranked 3, 4, and 5, respectively. Therefore, Aria ended up with 3 points, Danny with 2, and Taylor with 4 (clue 3).

Who can end up with 0 points? Not Aria, Danny, or Taylor, whose point totals are known; not Cheryl, who won in round 1 (clue 5); and not Gordon, who had at least a point from two draws (clue 7). Steven lost all his games. Steven, therefore, was not the undefeated player, and neither was Aria or Danny (who lost in round 1, per clue 5), nor Cheryl (who lost to Aria in round 4, per clue 6), nor the highest-scoring player Taylor (clue 1), so it was Gordon.

Taylor must have lost a game (clue 1), and must have lost it to Gordon (since Taylor won every other game to reach 4 points, and obviously did not win a game against an undefeated player). They met in round 5, since the other pairings for that round are known (the top two ranked armies of Aria and Danny met per clue 2, and Cheryl played Steven per clue 6). Taylor must have won four games in a row prior to round 5.

Gordon's win in round 5, two draws in rounds 3 and 4 (clue 7), and win against Steven in round 1 (since Steven lost all his games) mean that he had a draw in round 2 to reach 3.5 points, as per clue 4. Cheryl must be the player who ended up with 2.5 points.

Aria and Danny must be the pair who had a draw in round 5 per clue 7, since the other games are known to have ended decisively (Steven and Taylor losing to Cheryl and Gordon, respectively). Since Aria played Cheryl in round 4 (clue 6), her draw with Gordon was in round 3, and Danny and Gordon drew in round 4. By elimination, Aria's second-round opponent was Steven, Gordon's second-round opponent was Cheryl, Cheryl's third-round opponent was Taylor, and Taylor's second-round opponent was Danny, who played Steven in round 3. Finally, Steven played Taylor in round 4. From the known point totals of all the players, the win-lose-draw results of the remaining games are easily determined.

Years earlier, Gordon had spent time determining the relative values of chess pieces—not just standard chess pieces, but ones that appear in various historical and modern chess variants. He found that the most important single factor was a piece's mobility,

which he judged by adding up the number of squares a piece would attack when placed on every possible square of an empty chessboard. A rook would attack 14 squares no matter its square, while a bishop would attack anywhere from 7 to 13 squares, with a weighted average of 9.5 squares. The ratio of 9.5 to 14 closely matches the traditionally accepted values of bishop and rook (3+ and 5); the fact that the bishop is confined to squares of one color seems unimportant. Another important evaluation factor is whether or not a piece can jump: Other pieces usually block some of the possible moves of a bishop or rook, but not a knight, which explains why the knight is almost as good as a bishop despite having lower total mobility on an empty board. Another factor is that forward moves are more effective than sideways or backwards moves, which is why a ferz is better than a wazir.

Gordon evaluated the pieces used in the fantasy chess armies as follows:

W: 1.35

F: 1.65 (a well-established value through centuries of play in shatranj, a forerunner of modern chess)

C: 2.7 (less than the knight because on average it will attack fewer squares from a random board square)

N: 3.2

B: 3.4

R: 5.1

F+W: 3.1

C+F: 4.4

N+W: 4.6

N+F: 4.9

B+W: 4.9

N+C: 6.1

R+F: 6.8

B+N: 7.2

R+N: 9.0

R+B: 9.2

Note that the combo pieces are worth roughly a pawn more than the sum of their components, as is the case with the relative values of bishop, rook, and queen in chess.

Based on these values, the armies evaluate as follows: Aria 32.65, Cheryl 29.85, Danny 33.25, Gordon 30.9, Steven 30.7, and Taylor 32.4.

Puzzle 7.3: Seven, Zero

The word given by Taylor's replies is CITADEL. The alternative replies give the word DIALECT.

From Taylor's replies to INSTEAD and TACKLED, the letters A, D, E, and T must all be in the word; if one of those letters were not, the word would have to include three of the letters A, D, E, and T, plus the letters C, K, and L, and also two of the letters I, N, and S, adding up to eight letters. Therefore the word contains A, D, E, and T, two of the three letters C, K, and L, and one of the three letters I, N, and S.

CLOSING has three letters in common with the secret word, neither of which is the G or O. One match comes from I, N, or S, and so both C and L are found in the secret word. VICTORY contains the known matches C and T, and so its other match must come from the letter I.

The letters A, C, D, E, I, L, and T anagram to CITADEL and DIALECT. The more unusual DELTAIC also fits the letter patterns of Steven's answers.

Puzzle 7.4: Around Midnight

Brianna killed Kelly.

Aria sold *Whistler's Grandma* to Cheryl.
Brianna sold *Starry Knight* to Kelly.
Cheryl sold *The Screamer* to Taylor.
Danny sold *Garden of Early Delights* to Brianna.
Kelly sold *Persistence of Melody* to Steven.
Steven sold *Christina's Whirl* to Danny.
Taylor sold *American Goths* to Aria.

Danny and Kelly were in the art studio before midnight.
Aria and Steven were in the art studio after midnight.
Brianna and Steven were in the game alcove before midnight.
Brianna and Kelly were in the game alcove after midnight.
Aria and Taylor were in the guest wing before midnight.
Danny was in the guest wing after midnight.
Cheryl was on the screened porch from before midnight.
Cheryl and Taylor were on the screened porch after midnight.

The pairs of guests who had a buyer-seller relationship and who were together in one place after midnight were Kelly-Brianna and Cheryl-Taylor. Since Taylor's transactions are known to have been honest (clue 17), Brianna killed Kelly after midnight in the game alcove.

From clue 3, Aria, Brianna, Steven, and Taylor were the sellers of *American Goths*, *Christina's Whirl*, *Starry Knight*, and *Whistler's Grandma*, in come combination. From clue 4, Brianna, Kelly, Steven, and Taylor were the buyers of *Garden of Early Delights*, *Persistence of Melody*, *The Screamer*, and *Starry Knight*, in come combination.

   Neither Aria, Cheryl, nor Danny bought a painting from Cheryl, Danny, or Kelly since the former trio did not buy the paintings the latter group sold (*Garden of Early Delights*, *Persistence of Melody*, and *The Screamer*).

   The guest who bought *American Goths* and sold *Whistler's Grandma* per clue 6 can only be Aria, since neither Cheryl nor Danny sold *Whistler's Grandma* and the others did not buy *American Goths* (clues 3 and 4). From clue 5 and by elimination, Brianna sold *Starry Knight*, and so she was not the buyer of *Starry Knight*. By elimination, Kelly bought *Starry Knight* from Brianna.

   Since only Cheryl and Danny can have bought *Christina's Whirl* and *Whistler's Grandma*, Kelly did not sell *The Screamer* (clue 14). From clue 7, Kelly (buyer of *Starry Knight*) did not sell *Garden of Early Delights* and must have sold *Persistence of Melody*. Since Brianna sold to Kelly, Kelly did not sell to Brianna (clue 1), and so Brianna did not buy *Persistence of Melody*.

   From clue 7, Kelly was in the art studio before midnight with the seller of *Garden of Early Delights*, who (since there were no more than two guests in the same location at the same time, per clue 2) must be Danny rather than Cheryl (since, per clue 15, prior to going to the guest wing, he was in the art studio), and so Cheryl sold *The Screamer* and was on the screened porch before midnight (clue 12).

   From clue 16, Steven was in the game alcove before midnight and the art studio after midnight, since no one besides Danny and Kelly was in the art studio before midnight. From clue 8, Aria (buyer of *American Goths*) was in the art studio after midnight with the seller of *Christina's Whirl*, who therefore was Steven. By elimination, Taylor is the person who sold *American Goths* to Aria.

   From clue 9, Brianna (seller of *Starry Knight*) was in the game alcove before midnight with the buyer of *Persistence of Melody*, who was therefore Steven.

From clue 11, Aria (seller of *Whistler's Grandma*) was in the guest wing before midnight with the buyer of *The Screamer*. Since Brianna was in the game alcove before midnight, she did not buy *The Screamer* from Cheryl and so Taylor must have. By elimination, Brianna bought *Garden of Early Delights* from Danny.

   From clue 10, Kelly was in the game alcove after midnight. From clue 17, Taylor was on the screened porch after midnight (since from clue 11 Taylor was in the guest wing before midnight). Aria, Danny, Kelly, Steven, and Taylor are all known to have been in two different locations, which means that at midnight Brianna stayed in the game alcove and Cheryl stayed on the screened porch (clue 2).

   Since everyone else's whereabouts are accounted for, only Danny was in the guest wing after midnight, and so, per clue 13, Danny bought *Christina's Whirl* and Cheryl bought *Whistler's Grandma*.

Weekend 8

Puzzle 8.1: Who's Whose

Aria invited Rachel, a systems analyst, whose favorite TV series is *The 100*. They met at a 5K race.
Brianna invited Hugh, a bartender, whose favorite TV series is *The Americans*. They met at a political rally.
Danny invited Wendy, a video editor, whose favorite TV series is *Buffy the Vampire Slayer*. They met at a volleyball game.
Kelly invited John, a graphic artist, whose favorite TV series is *The Wire*. They met at an art museum.
Steven invited Morgan, an x-ray technician whose favorite TV series is *Friday Night Lights*. They met at a nature center.

From clue 2, the graphic artist, systems editor, and x-ray technician first met the guests who invited them at 5K race, art museum, and nature center, in some combination.

   From clue 3, Aria, Danny, and Steven invited people whose favorite TV series are *Buffy the Vampire Slayer*, *Friday Night Lights*, and *The 100*, in some combination.

   From clue 4, the favorite TV series of Hugh, John, and Wendy are *The Americans*, *Buffy the Vampire Slayer*, and *The Wire*, in some combination.

   From clue 5, the favorite TV series of the bartender, the systems analyst, and the video editor are *The Americans*, *Buffy the Vampire Slayer*, and *The 100*, in some combination.

   From clue 6, Hugh, Morgan, and Rachel are the bartender, systems analyst, and x-ray technician, in some combination.

   From clue 7, Aria, Brianna, and Kelly first met their invitees at a 5K race, art museum, and political rally, in some combination.

   From clue 8, Brianna, Danny, and Steven invited the bartender, the x-ray technician, and the video editor, in some combination.

   From clues 2 and 5, the invitees whose favorite TV series were *Friday Night Lights* and *The Wire* did not first meet the guest who invited them at a political rally or a volleyball game.

   From clues 3 and 4, neither Brianna nor Kelly invited either Morgan or Rachel.

   From clues 3 and 7, the favorite TV series of the invitee who was first met at a nature center was neither *The Americans* nor *The Wire*, and *The Americans* was not the favorite TV series of the invitee who was first met at a volleyball game.

   From clues 2 and 8, neither Aria nor Kelly met their invitee at a political rally, since neither the graphic artist nor the systems analyst was met there. By elimination, Brianna's invitee was first met at a political rally and has the favorite series *The Americans* (other choices having already been ruled out by clues 2, 3, and 5), and Kelly's invitee's favorite series is *The Wire*. Since Aria did not meet her invitee at an art museum (clue 9), by elimination she met her invitee at a 5K race, and Kelly's invitee was first met at an art museum.

Since the systems analyst's favorite series is not *The Wire* (clue 5), Kelly's invitee cannot be the system analyst and by elimination is the graphic artist, whose favorite series is *The Wire*. This means that the system analyst is Aria's invitee, whom she met at a 5K race. By elimination, *Friday Night Lights* is the favorite series of the x-ray technician, who was met at the nature center (since the graphic artist was met at the art museum). *The Americans* is not the systems analyst's favorite series (since *The Americans* is the favorite series of Brianna's invitee), nor is it the video editor's (clue 10), so by elimination it is the bartender's favorite series. Since the bartender met Brianna at a political rally, the video editor met his or her inviting guest at a volleyball game.

Since Brianna invited the bartender, but neither John nor Wendy has that job (clue 6), the bartender is Hugh, whose favorite series is *The Americans* and whom Brianna met at a political rally. From clue 11 and by elimination, John's favorite series is *The Wire*, and so John is the graphic artist met by Kelly at the art museum. By elimination, Wendy is the video editor invited by Danny (not by Steven, per clue 10), whom she first met at a volleyball game, and Steven invited the x-ray technician. Wendy's favorite series is *Buffy the Vampire Slayer*. Rachel is the systems analyst whose favorite series is *The 100*.

Since Morgan was not met at a 5K race (clue 11), Aria invited Rachel and Steven invited Morgan.

Puzzle 8.2: Thrill Island Excursion

The people, their favorite rides, and the foods they ate, were as follows:

Aria, Teacups, churro and soft pretzel
Brianna, Caterpillar, corn dog and fried cheese curds
Cheryl, Loop-the-Loop, churro and cotton candy
Danny, Gyro Tower, corn dog and soft pretzel
Gordon, Tunnel of Love, funnel cake and soft pretzel
Hugh, Octopus, churro and corn dog
John, Octopus, cotton candy and fried cheese curds
Kelly, Loop-the-Loop, corn dog and funnel cake
Morgan, Gyro Tower, churro and funnel cake
Nina, Tunnel of Love, corn dog and cotton candy
Nolan, Loop-the-Loop, fried cheese curds and soft pretzel
Rachel, Caterpillar, cotton candy and soft pretzel
Steven, Teacups, fried cheese curds and funnel cake
Taylor, Log Flume, churro and fried cheese curds
Wendy, Round Up, cotton candy and funnel cake

From clues 4, 5, and 6, the Loop-the-Loop was three people's favorite ride, the Log Flume and Round Up were favored by one person each, and the other rides were each the favorites of two people. Besides the possible favorite rides eliminated by those three clues, per clue 7, Aria's and Danny's favorites weren't the Caterpillar or Tunnel of Love, Morgan's and Steven's favorites weren't the Octopus or Round Up, Brianna's and Gordon's favorites weren't the Gyro Tower or Teacups, and Nina's and Rachel's favorites weren't the Log Flume or Octopus.

Per clue 13, Nina's favorite ride wasn't the Loop-the-Loop, so it isn't Gordon's favorite ride either (clue 7).

Setting aside favorite rides for now, let's look at the snacks. Exactly 15 combinations of two foods can be made from a set of six foods, and so from clue 2, every possible combination was used by

one guest, which also means that every food was eaten by exactly five different guests. Clues 8 and 9 indicate the snacks eaten by the guests who favored Log Flume and Round Up, and clues 14, 15, and 16 indicate a few individual snacks eaten by some of the guests. Since John had fried cheese curds, his favorite ride wasn't Round Up, and since his favorite ride wasn't Log Flume, his other snack wasn't a churro. Since Taylor had fried cheese curds, Taylor's favorite ride wasn't Tunnel of Love (clue 17).

Clues 10, 11, and 12 indicate groups of five people who all ate the same snack. Let's call them groups A, B, and C, respectively. We know that exactly five people had each snack, so we can eliminate any snack from consideration that was eaten by anyone not in the group. Given that, group A can only have eaten churros, corn dogs, or cotton candy. Group B can only have eaten corn dogs or cotton candy (churros aren't possible since John didn't have a churro). Group C can only have eaten churros, corn dogs, cotton candy, or funnel cake.

The person whose favorite ride was Round Up has been narrowed down to Nolan and Wendy. If Nolan's favorite ride was Round Up, then he had cotton candy and funnel cake. Since Nolan is not in group A, B, or C, that would eliminate cotton candy and funnel cake as possibilities for all three, leaving only churros and corn dogs, which isn't enough for all three groups. Wendy, therefore, must be the one whose favorite was Round Up, and she had cotton candy and funnel cake, which must represent group B and group C respectively (since Gordon, in group C, had funnel cake per clue 16).

Since no combinations of snacks were repeated, anyone who ate cotton candy besides John didn't have fried cheese curds, and anyone who ate cotton candy besides Rachel didn't have a soft pretzel. Brianna, Morgan, and Steven also didn't have soft pretzels per clues 3 and 7. Brianna isn't in group A, so whichever food was eaten by group A, either churros or corn dogs, Brianna didn't have it, so by elimination she must have had fried cheese curds, which means she didn't ride the Tunnel of Love and neither did Rachel (clue 17). Brianna's favorite ride wasn't the log flume, so she didn't have a churro with her fried cheese curds, and she must have had a corn dog, which means group A had churros.

Taylor, then, had a churro and fried cheese curds, so Taylor is the one who favored the Log Flume. By elimination, since Nolan didn't have a corn dog (clue 18), Nolan had fried cheese curds and a soft pretzel, and Nina had a corn dog with her cotton candy. Hugh didn't have a soft pretzel with his churro (since Aria had that combo), and Gordon didn't have a corn dog (since Nina did, and they shared the same favorite ride). Hugh didn't have fried cheese curds with his churro (since Taylor had that combo), so he had a corn dog.

Brianna and Rachel had the same favorite ride, which was either Caterpillar or Loop-the-Loop, and together they ate a corn dog, cotton candy, fried cheese curds, and a soft pretzel. If their favorite ride was Loop-the-Loop, then the third person who most liked that ride must have eaten a churro and funnel cake, but that's what Morgan had, and since Morgan and Danny had the same favorite ride (clue 7), that would make too many people who favored Loop-the-Loop. Brianna and Rachel, therefore, both liked the Caterpillar most, and by elimination Gordon and Nina's shared favorite ride was the Tunnel of Love. Gordon didn't have fried cheese curds (clue 17), so he was the fifth person to have a soft pretzel. Danny didn't have fried cheese curds with his soft pretzel (since Nolan had that combo), so Danny had a corn dog. Since neither Danny nor Morgan had fried cheese curds, their shared favorite ride wasn't Teacups (clue 17). If their shared favorite was Loop-the-Loop, their snack selections of a churro, corn dog, funnel cake, and soft pretzel would mean the other Loop-the-Loop lover was John, who had cotton candy and fried cheese curds. But John is in the clue 6 group with Morgan, so this is impossible, and Danny and Morgan both favored Gyro Tower.

Either Aria or Cheryl rode Loop-the-Loop, and both had a churro, so Hugh didn't ride Loop-the-Loop, since he also had a churro, and by elimination he rode Octopus and Kelly rode Loop-the-Loop (clue 5). Since Kelly had funnel cake, Steven (who also had funnel cake) didn't favor Loop-the-Loop, and by elimination his favorite ride was Teacups, as was Aria's. Aria didn't have fried cheese curds, so Steven must have (clue 17), and by elimination Kelly had a corn dog with her funnel cake. By elimination, Cheryl's favorite ride was Loop-the-Loop. The two snacks that she and Kelly didn't eat were fried cheese curds and a soft pretzel, which Nolan had, so Nolan is the third who favored Loop-the-Loop and John's favorite was Octopus.

Puzzle 8.3: Paintball

Players were eliminated in the following order:

Hugh was eliminated by Danny.
Brianna was eliminated by Rachel.
Steven was eliminated by Nolan.
Wendy was eliminated by Cheryl.
John was eliminated by Kelly.
Aria was eliminated by Morgan.
Rachel was eliminated by Danny.
Danny was eliminated by Morgan.
Cheryl was eliminated by Nolan.
Morgan was eliminated by Kelly.
Kelly was eliminated by Nolan, who was the last person standing.

From clues 1 and 2, the sequence of eliminations includes Brianna followed by four people followed by Rachel, Danny, Morgan, and Kelly, with others possibly before Brianna and/or in between or after the last four. Therefore, Brianna was eliminated first, second, or third; Rachel was sixth, seventh, or eighth; Danny was seventh, eighth, or ninth; Morgan was eighth, ninth, or tenth; and Kelly was ninth, tenth, or eleventh, or was never eliminated. From clue 3, Nolan was not among the first six people eliminated.

From clue 2, since Morgan was the eighth, ninth, or tenth person eliminated, Steven was first, second, or third. Rachel cannot have been sixth, since then at most four people could have been eliminated between her and Hugh, and so Rachel was seventh or eighth, Hugh was first or second, and Brianna (with four players eliminated between her and Rachel) cannot have been first. Brianna, Steven, and Hugh account for first, second, and third in some order, so no one else was eliminated in those positions. Since Brianna was eliminated second or third, Aria was eliminated sixth or seventh. Since Danny eliminated Rachel (clue 1), Danny was not seventh; since Morgan eliminated Danny, Morgan was not eighth; and since Kelly eliminated Morgan, Kelly was not ninth. Since Morgan was not eighth, Steven was not first, so by elimination Hugh was eliminated first, and so Rachel was eliminated seventh. which means Brianna was eliminated second, Aria was sixth, and by elimination Steven was third. Morgan's relative position to Steven means he was eliminated tenth, and so Kelly was either eliminated eleventh or not at all.

There were four players between Cheryl and Wendy (clue 2). The only positions not accounted for are fourth, fifth, eighth, ninth, and eleventh, and the only ones with four positions between them

are fourth and ninth, so Cheryl and Wendy were eliminated in those positions in some order. Danny, then, wasn't eliminated ninth and was eighth instead. By elimination, Nolan was eliminated eleventh or not at all, and John must have been eliminated fifth, as everyone else has been ruled out from that position. Per clue 4, either Cheryl or Danny eliminated Wendy (she wasn't eliminated by Morgan or Nolan, who were on her team); if Cheryl was fourth and Wendy was ninth, then Cheryl and Danny would both have been eliminated before Wendy, which is impossible, so Wendy was fourth and Cheryl was ninth.

Since Morgan eliminated Danny, Morgan also eliminated Aria, who was eliminated sixth (clue 5 and the fact that Morgan was eliminated tenth by Kelly). Per clue 3, then, Steven was eliminated by Nolan.

Danny eliminated one of the last seven players (Rachel, eliminated seventh), so Kelly, Morgan, and Nolan each eliminated two of the others (clue 3). Both of Morgan's eliminations in that group are accounted for (Aria and Danny, sixth and eighth respectively), as is one of Kelly's (Morgan, eliminated tenth). John, eliminated fifth, can't have been eliminated by his teammate Nolan, so Kelly eliminated John, and the other two eliminations must both have been by Nolan: Cheryl, eliminated ninth, and the final elimination, which must have been Kelly.

Per clue 4, Hugh and Wendy were eliminated by Cheryl and Danny in some order. But since Danny eliminated someone before Rachel did (clue 6) and Rachel's only elimination was Brianna, Danny eliminated Hugh and Cheryl eliminated Wendy.

Weekend 9

Puzzle 9.1: Card-Jackers

Aria, Kelly, and Taylor are the thieves. Taylor's statement is true, but Aria's and Kelly's are false.

Per clue 1, there were fewer than four thieves. If there were one or two thieves, there would be more false statements than thieves, which is impossible, so there were three thieves, and Kelly's statement is false and she is guilty.

If Danny's statement is false, then Kelly and Steven are both lying. (It is possible for a guilty party to tell the truth, but Steven claims to be innocent, so if he's guilty, then he's lying.) In that case, Danny, Kelly, and Steven would all be guilty, but then impossible for everyone else to be innocent and telling the truth (in fact, in this hypothetical, they would all have to be lying), so Danny's statement is true (and he is innocent, per clue 2), and Steven is innocent and telling the truth, which means Cheryl is telling the truth.

If Aria's statement is true, either Brianna or Cheryl is guilty and the other is innocent. If Brianna is the guilty one, then Brianna's statement is true, but she can't make a true statement unless she is innocent (clue 2), so this is impossible. If Cheryl is the guilty one, then Brianna's statement is a lie, which means Brianna would also be guilty, which is a contradiction. Aria's statement, then, must be false, and she is guilty.

For Aria's statement to be false, Brianna and Cheryl must either be both guilty or both innocent. If they are both guilty, then there would be four guilty guests, contradicting clue 1, so they are both innocent. By elimination, Taylor must be guilty of being the remaining thief despite making a true statement.

Puzzle 9.2: Shady Shamuses

Steven killed Nolan.

Five years ago:
Aria investigated Kelly for insurance fraud.
Brianna investigated Nolan for hiding assets.
Cheryl investigated Danny for toxic waste dumping.
Danny investigated Brianna for money laundering.
Kelly investigated Steven for tax evasion.
Nolan investigated Cheryl for blackmail.
Steven investigated Taylor for embezzlement.
Taylor investigated Aria for murder.

This year:
Aria has investigated Brianna for hiding assets.
Brianna has investigated Danny for insurance fraud.
Cheryl has investigated Kelly for tax evasion.
Danny has investigated Aria for toxic waste dumping.
Kelly has investigated Taylor for embezzlement.
Nolan has investigated Steven for murder.
Steven has investigated Nolan for blackmail.
Taylor has investigated Cheryl for money laundering.

From clue 9, Brianna, Cheryl, Danny, and Nolan investigated one another five years ago, in some combination, and this year, Cheryl, Kelly, Nolan, Steven, and Taylor have been investigating each other in some combination. From clues 3 and 4, no one other than Nolan, Steven, or Taylor investigated blackmail, embezzlement, or murder five years ago. Similarly, no one other than the people named in clues 5, 6, and 15 investigated the crimes mentioned in those clues in the year mentioned. (Specifically, five years ago, Aria and Danny investigated insurance fraud and money laundering, and this year, Aria, Danny, and Kelly investigated embezzlement, hiding assets, and toxic waste dumping.)

Since, five years ago, Nolan did not investigate insurance fraud, money laundering, or tax evasion (clue 4), he did not investigate Brianna at that time (clue 10). For the same reason, neither Steven nor Taylor investigated Kelly at that time, nor did Taylor investigate Steven. By elimination, Taylor investigated Aria five years ago, and by further elimination, five years ago Steven investigated Taylor, Kelly investigated Steven, and Aria investigated Kelly. This means that this year Kelly and Steven have not been investigating Steven and Taylor, respectively (clue 1).

From clues 5 and 10, Kelly investigated Steven for tax evasion five years ago. Cheryl could not have investigated Brianna at that time, since none of the crimes Cheryl could have been investigating match the ones for which Brianna could have been investigated (clues 5 and 10). By elimination, Danny investigated Brianna five years ago, which means he did not investigate her this year (clue 1). By elimination, this year Danny has been investigating Aria, Brianna has been investigating Danny, and Aria has been investigating Brianna. Brianna therefore did not investigate Danny five years ago.

Brianna has been investigating Danny this year for insurance fraud, the only crime in common between clues 6 and 12. Per the same clues, neither Nolan nor Steven has been investigating Kelly this year; and neither Kelly, Nolan, nor Steven has been investigating Cheryl this year. By elimination, Taylor has been investigating Cheryl this year. By further elimination, Cheryl has been investigating Kelly this year, Nolan has been investigating Steven, Steven has been investigating Nolan (and thus is the killer, per clue 2), and Kelly has been investigating Taylor. From clue 13, Taylor investigated murder five years ago.

From clue 11, Cheryl investigated Danny rather than Nolan five years ago, since Nolan did not investigate money laundering at that time, and since Danny therefore was investigating money laundering, Aria can only have been investigating insurance fraud. By elimination, Nolan investigated Cheryl five years ago, and Brianna was investigating Nolan. Since Steven did not investigate blackmail that year (clue 14), Nolan did, and Steven investigated embezzlement. Since Nolan investigated blackmail five years ago, he did not do so this year, and so Steven did. By elimination, Nolan was investigating murder this year.

The three people who could be investigating hiding assets this year are Aria, Danny, and Kelly, who are, respectively, investigating Brianna, Aria, and Taylor. Per clue 7, since neither Aria nor Taylor investigated hiding assets five years ago, Aria must be the one who is investigating hiding assets this year, and Brianna investigated hiding assets five years ago. By elimination, five years ago Cheryl investigated toxic waste dumping.

Either Danny or Kelly is investigating someone this year for embezzlement. From clue 8, since Danny's target, Aria, is investigating hiding assets, Kelly must be investigating Taylor for embezzlement, and Taylor's investigation of Cheryl is for money laundering. By elimination, Cheryl is investigating Kelly for tax evasion and Danny is investigating Aria for toxic waste dumping.

Puzzle 9.3: Curio Cabinet

	1	2	3	4	5	6
A	gorillA	Bat	Cow			Dolphin
B	vulturE			Fox	Gorilla	ostricH
C	kiwI	Jaguar	Kiwi	quaiL	Monkey	dolphiN
D		Ostrich	sheeP	Quail		
E		jaguaR	Sheep		baT	zebU
F	Vulture		coW	foX	monkeY	Zebu

First, it is useful to note the order in which the animals are placed in the cabinet: gorillA, Bat, Cow, Dolphin, vulturE, Fox, Gorilla, ostricH, kiwI, Jaguar, Kiwi, quaiL, Monkey, dolphiN, Ostrich, sheeP, Quail, jaguaR, Sheep, baT, zebU, Vulture, coW, foX, monkeY, Zebu. We've labeled the rows of the cabinet A to F from top to bottom, and the columns of the cabinet 1 to 6 from left to right, for easy reference.

Let's start by examining clue 6. Both ostriches precede both sheep in their order of placement in the cabinet. The earliest possible position of the first ostrich—let's call it ostrich 1—is in cubbyhole B4 (not B3, because there must be at least one empty cubbyhole in row A, per clue 2). The two kiwis after ostrich 1 are in the same row (clue 4), so kiwi 1 can't be in row B since there isn't room for kiwi 2 in that row, so kiwi 1 is placed no earlier than cubbyhole C1. The two kiwis aren't in row D, because there are at most 15 animals in the bottom three rows (clue 2), so all animals before quail 1 must be in the top three rows. Since both kiwis are in row C, the latest possible placement for ostrich 1 is C3. Row C is full, so dolphin 2 is placed no earlier than C6, and ostrich 2 is in D1 or later. The pair of sheep are in different rows (clue 4), and there are too many animals after sheep 2 for it to be placed any later than E4, so sheep 1 is in row D and ostrich 2 is somewhere in the range D1 to D5.

Ostrich 2 can't be in D3; if it were, sheep 2 would be in E2 or E4, and in neither position is there any possible way for ostrich 1 to intersect with the other diagonal through that cubbyhole. If ostrich 2 were in D4 or D5, sheep 2 would be in E3 or E4, with ostrich 1 in C1 or C2. The pair of sheep, then, could not be in the same column. Per clue 7, nine of the thirteen pairs of animals share a column with each other. Per clue 4, the kiwis cannot be in the same column. Per clue 5, the gorillas cannot be in the same column. And as we have seen from our exploration of clue 6, the ostriches cannot be in the same column either, because they intersect two different diagonals crossing through a cubbyhole in row E, and are both above row E. That's three pairs of animals that don't share the same column, and so at most one other pair of animals does not share a column. If the sheep don't share a column, then every other animal besides kiwis, gorillas, and ostriches does. So let's see if that's possible.

Zebu 1 must be higher than zebu 2 no matter what (clue 4), so zebu 1 is in row E. In this scenario, sheep 2 is in E3 or E4, and bat 2 is between sheep 2 and zebu 1, so that would place it in E4 or E5 and zebu 1 in E5 or E6. If the two bats must share a column, bat 1 in the top row must be in column 4 or 5. Zebu 1 is followed by vulture 2 and cow 2, so cow 2 would be, at the earliest, in cubbyhole F1, so cow 1 would have to be in B1, at the earliest, to share a column with it. Fox 2 is, at the latest, in F4. If cow 1 is in B1, then the dolphin-vulture-fox sequence must fill B2-B3-B4 for the foxes to share a column. (Fox 1 must precede C3, the latest possible position for ostrich 1.) But vulture 2 is between zebu 2 and cow 2, so there's no way to get it into column 3. This hypothetical, then, is impossible, and ostrich 2 must therefore be in D1 or D2, with sheep 2 in E2 or E3 and ostrich 1 in B5 or B6. Kiwi 1 is the first animal after ostrich 1, and we've already shown it's in row C, so we can fill in all of row C, per clue 2: kiwi 1, jaguar 1, kiwi 2, quail 1, monkey 1, dolphin 2.

Let's look at clue 5 now. Bat 1 is in row A with gorilla 1 (per clue 3, and also per the number of animals that must fit before ostrich 1), so it's not the bat referred to in this clue. Bat 2 is the next animal after sheep 2 in E2 or E3, so it's in E3 or later. Six other animals follow bat 2, so it's placed no later than E5 (there is at least one empty cubbyhole in row F, per clue 2). Assume gorilla 2 is the gorilla it shares a diagonal with. Gorilla 2 is not in row A (since there are six animals before it) and is somewhere before ostrich 1 (in B5 or B6), so it's somewhere in the range from B1 to B5. For gorilla 2 and bat 2 to share a diagonal, gorilla 2 must be three columns to the left of bat 2. Gorilla 1 would then have to be directly above bat 2, which would only leave two cubbyholes between gorilla 1 and gorilla 2, which is obviously not enough cubbyholes. Gorilla 1 and bat 2, then, share a diagonal, and can only be in A1 and E5 respectively, with gorilla 2 in B5, in the same column with bat 2. Since gorilla 2 is taking up cubbyhole B5, ostrich 1 must be in B6, which places sheep 2 in E3 and ostrich 2 in D2. The zebus don't share a row (as we've shown per clue 4), so zebu 1 is in E6.

Given the animals left to fit in row F, cow 2 is in F2 or F3. Cow 1 is in A3 at the earliest and A6 at the latest. (It's not in B1 since that would fill row B, contradictory to clue 2.) If the bats share a column, bat 1 would be in A5 and cow 1 in A6, so the cows could not also share a column. If the cows share a column, cow 1 must

be in A3 (with cow 2 in F3) and bat 1 in A2, so the bats could not share a column. Since it's impossible for both the bat and cow pairs to share columns, and we've already identified three other animals that don't share a column (kiwis, gorillas, and ostriches), every other animal pair besides bats and cows must share a column. This means we have a few easy placements we can make: sheep 1 in D3 (paired with E3), monkey 2 in F5 (paired with C5), and zebu 2 in F6 (paired with E6). Quail 2 precedes sheep 2, so it must be in D4 (paired with C4). Dolphin 1 can only pair with dolphin 2 in C6 if it's placed in A6. Bat 1 isn't adjacent to dolphin 1 (cow 1 is between them), so the bats don't share a column, which means the cows do, so the cows are in A3 and F3, and bat 1 is in A2. Fox 2 is in F4, between cow 2 and monkey 2, so fox 1 is in B4.

Jaguar 2 must be in E2 (paired with C2). This leaves only the vultures to place, and since each column contains at least one pair (clue 7), they must be in B1 and F1, since it's the only remaining column with no pair in it.

Puzzle 9.4: All the Marbles

Given groups of three, five, and eight marbles, a player should choose to go first and to remove two marbles from the group of eight, leaving groups of three, five, and six. Whatever marble(s) the next player removes, it will be possible for the player who went first to create another "zero" position, meaning a position in which whoever goes next will lose.

The easiest way to analyze this is by writing the number of marbles in each group as binary (base 2) numbers, where the digits from right to left represent 1's, 2's, 4's, 8's, and so forth, like this (with some extra zeros put in front of the first two numbers to make the columns clearer):

> 3 in binary is 0011
> 5 in binary is 0101
> 8 in binary is 1000

There are two 1's in the 1's column, and these cancel one another out. What the first player on move 1 must do is to bring about an even number of 1's in the other columns. Since only the 8 has a 1 in the 8's column, that number must be reduced, and in such a way that what is left cancels the 1's in the 2's and 4's columns. After removing two marbles, the result is this:

> 3 in binary is 011
> 5 in binary is 101
> 6 in binary is 110

Now there are pairs of 1's in every column. Whichever column or columns the next player disturbs the balance in, it's just a matter of finding a way to restore the balance and keep an even number of 1's in each column. It will always be possible.

Weekend 10

Puzzle 10.1: Bridge Pros

Aria plans to kill Danny.

Brianna, Kelly, and Steven use Standard American bidding; Cheryl, Danny, and Kelly bid a Strong Club system; and Aria, Cheryl, and Steven play Two-Over-One.

The pairs as ranked by the Montagues, and the city where each pair had a recent win, are as follows:

#1 Brianna and Kelly, Indianapolis
#2 Cheryl and Kelly, Denver
#3 Danny and Kelly, Honolulu
#4 Cheryl and Danny, Pittsburgh
#5 Brianna and Steven, Nashville
#6 Aria and Cheryl, Austin
#7 Kelly and Steven, St. Louis
#8 Cheryl and Steven, Phoenix
#9 Aria and Steven, Las Vegas

If there were no murder, the Montagues' first choices would be the pairs Brianna-Kelly and Cheryl-Danny. (Cheryl-Kelly and Danny-Kelly are precluded by Kelly's being partnered with Brianna.)

If Aria or Steven kills Brianna, the top available pair would be Cheryl-Kelly and the only other pair available would be Aria and Steven. The sum of their rankings is 2 + 9 = 11.

If Aria or Steven kills Cheryl, the top pair available would be Brianna-Kelly and the only other pair available would be Aria and Steven. The sum of their rankings is 1 + 9 = 10.

If Steven kills Kelly, the top two pairs would be Cheryl-Danny and Brianna-Steven. The sum of their rankings is 4 + 5 = 9.

If Aria kills Danny, the top two pairs would be Brianna-Kelly and Aria-Cheryl. The sum of their rankings is 1 + 6 = 7. This is the lowest total of any valid scenario. (If Steven killed Danny, he would not end up on the Montagues' team, so that possibility is ruled out by clue 15.)

Three pros play each bidding system (clue 2), making possible three different pairings of pros using that system (e.g., players A, B, and C can form the partnerships A-B, A-C, and B-C.) In order to account for all nine partnerships mentioned in clue 1, every pro must have been paired once with every other pro who plays the same bidding system.

From clues 3, 4, and 5, Brianna and Kelly bid Standard American, Cheryl and Danny bid Strong Club, and Aria and Steven bid Two-Over-One. Any player who only bids one system can be part of at most two pairings, and since, per clues 6, 7, and 8, Kelly, Steven, and Cheryl all played more than two events, they are the three who played two systems, and Aria, Brianna, and Danny played no other systems than the ones given in clues 3, 4, and 5.

The third person bidding Standard American, then, must be Cheryl or Steven. If it's Cheryl, then per clue 3 she is also in a pairing with Aria—but Aria only bids Two-Over-One, so Cheryl would then need to play all three bidding strategies, which is impossible (clue 2). Steven, then, is the third Standard American bidder, and won in Las Vegas with Aria, where they must have bid Two-Over-One. By elimination, Cheryl bids Two-Over-One (and won in Denver, per clue 5) and Kelly bids Strong Club (and won in Indianapolis, per clue 4). Since neither of the other Strong Club bidders won in Indianapolis, Kelly must have bid Standard American there with either Brianna or Steven.

Per clues 6 and 8, the 2nd-ranked pair is Cheryl and Kelly (for which they bid Strong Club), and per clues 7 and 8 the 8th-ranked pair is Steven and Cheryl (for which they bid Two-Over-One).

From clue 9, the pairs that won in Austin, Denver, Honolulu, Indianapolis, and Las Vegas finished 1st, 2nd, 3rd, 6th, and 9th in some combination. From clue 10, Indianapolis finished 1st or 2nd and Denver finished 2nd or 3rd. But since Cheryl finished 2nd and she didn't win in Indianapolis, Indianapolis is 1st and Cheryl and Kelly's 2nd-place win bidding Strong Club was in Denver. Aria and Steven's victory in Las Vegas playing Two-Over-One was not 3rd (since Kelly played that game) or 6th (since Cheryl played that one), so it was 9th. Since Steven plays Two-Over-One in the pairs ranked 8th and 9th, his pair ranked 7th plays Standard American.

The Austin and Honolulu winners are ranked 3rd and 6th in some order. From clue 12, the Honolulu winners are ranked 3rd, the Pittsburgh winners 4th, the Nashville winners 5th, and the Austin winners 6th.

Cheryl's pair ranked 4th uses a Strong Club system (clue 11), and her pairing with Kelly is 2nd, so she paired at 4th with the other Strong Club player, Danny. By elimination, she paired with Aria in 6th, playing Two-Over-One, which accounts for all three Two-Over-One games.

The winning pairs in Nashville and St. Louis used the same bidding system (clue 13). Since the Nashville game in 5th didn't use Two-Over-One, the St. Louis game wasn't 8th and must have been 7th, and by elimination Phoenix was 8th. Steven bid Standard American in 7th, so the Nashville game in 5th was also Standard American, and by elimination, the 3rd-place game was Strong Club, and so Kelly's partner for that game must have been Danny.

Brianna's pairs were in two of the positions 1st, 5th, and 7th. But Kelly was not in the 8th- or 9th-place pairs, so Brianna's second-highest pairing can't be 7th (clue 14) which means she finished 1st (with Kelly) and 5th. By elimination, her 5th-place win was with Steven, and Steven's 7th-place win was with Kelly.

Puzzle 10.2: Bridge Amateurs

The partnerships and their net IMP scores were:
Cheryl and Kelly outscored their opponents by 19.
Danny and Nolan outscored their opponents by 13.
Brianna and Taylor were outscored by 1 by their opponents.
Aria and Steven were outscored by 31 by their opponents.

The team results were as follows:
Match 1: Brianna–Taylor and Danny–Nolan defeated Aria–Steven and Cheryl–Kelly by 6 IMPs.
Match 2: Brianna–Taylor and Cheryl–Kelly defeated Aria–Steven and Danny–Nolan by 9 IMPs.
Match 3: Cheryl–Kelly and Danny–Nolan defeated Aria–Steven and Brianna–Taylor by 16 IMPs.

Since the number of IMPs by which partnerships outscored their opponents must balance the number by which partnerships were outscored, the score not given in clues 1, 6, and 8 must be 19 IMPs. Since 19 is higher than all the given scores, it must be Cheryl's team's winning score, which they earned despite losing their first match (clue 3).

In this tournament structure, if one pair wins all its matches, the other pairs will each win one (the match in which it is teamed with the winner) and lose two (the other two matches). Similarly, if one pair loses all its matches, the other pairs will each win two and lose one. (It's impossible for there to be an outcome in which one team doesn't either win or lose three games.) Since Cheryl's team won the tournament but lost one match, there can't have been another team that won all three matches, or they would have beaten Cheryl's team, so someone lost all three matches, and it must be Aria's team, who had the lowest score (clue 1). Every other pair, then, won two and lost one.

Steven lost his last two matches (clue 7), and since every team besides Aria's lost only one match, he must be Aria's partner. Cheryl, Nolan, and Taylor had three different scores (clues 1, 6, and 8), so they were on three different teams, paired with Brianna, Danny, and Kelly in some combination.

Cheryl lost her first match, so she must have won both her second and third matches (since every pair except Aria's won two matches), which means she didn't partner with Danny, who lost the second match (clue 4) or Brianna, who lost the third match (clue 2). By elimination, then, Kelly was Cheryl's partner. Since Danny lost the second match, his partner wasn't Taylor, who won that match (clue 5), so his partner was Nolan. By elimination, Taylor's partner was Brianna.

The margins of victory in the three matches can be determined from the pairs' final scores. The problem amounts to finding three numbers that, when added and/or subtracted from one another, add up to 19, 13, –1, and –31. Let a, b, and c stand for the winning margins in the first, second, and third matches, respectively. The Aria–Steven score can be written as the equation $-31 = -(a+b+c)$. Since Brianna and Taylor were partners who lost only the third match, their score can be written as the equation $a+b-c = -1$. This can be rewritten as $a+b = c-1$. Substituting $c-1$ for $a+b$ in the Aria-Steven equation yields $-31 = -(c-1+c)$, or $31 = 2c-1$, and so $c = 16$. Using an equation for the Danny–Nolan score, $a-b+c = 13$, and putting in the value for c, we know that $a-b = -3$; and since $a+b = 15$, we can easily determine that $a = 6$ and $b = 9$.

Puzzle 10.3: Knickknacks

The beaked whale is in the lounge and is made of wood.
The beluga is in the library and is made of wood.
The blue whale is in the sitting room and is made of metal.
The grey whale is in the lounge and is made of metal.
The humpback whale is in the master bedroom and is made of glass.
The narwhal is in the private study and is made of glass.
The right whale is in the library and is made of glass.
The rorqual is in the dining room and is made of wood.
The sperm whale is in the master bedroom and is made of metal.

Since the sitting room contains only one whale (clue 1), only the blue whale, grey whale, or humpback whale can be there (clue 5). Since the dining room and private study each contain only one whale, only the narwhal, right whale, or rorqual can be in those rooms (clue 6). From clue 7, the beaked whale and beluga are in the library and lounge in some combination. One of the whales in clue 5 is in the master bedroom; the other whale in that room isn't the beaked whale or beluga, nor any of the whales in clue 6, so the sperm whale must be in the master bedroom.

From clues 2, 3, and 4, the metal whales are in the lounge, master bedroom, and sitting room, and the wood whales are in the dining room, library, and lounge. From clues 6 and 10, since the right whale and rorqual are in rooms without a metal whale, the sperm whale must be metal.

From clue 8, the blue and grey whales must be metal, since it is the only material common to the whales in any of the three rooms they can occupy, per clue 5. The glass whale in the master bedroom must be the humpback whale.

The beaked whale and beluga must both be wood (clue 7), the only material in common between the library and lounge.

That only leaves one wood whale unaccounted for, so the shared material of the narwhal and right whale (clue 9) must be glass, and the rorqual is wood and is in the dining room. (It's not in the library, since the beaked whale or beluga accounts for the wood whale in that room.)

Clue 11 pinpoints the beluga as being in the library. By elimination, the beaked whale is in the lounge.

Clue 12 pinpoints the blue whale as being in the sitting room and the narwhal as being in the private study, which places the grey whale in the lounge and the right whale in the library.

Puzzle 10.4: Mental Blocks

Aria had group B and finished fourth.
Brianna had group G and finished fifth.
Cheryl had group C and finished second.
Danny had group A and finished third.
Kelly had group E and finished sixth.
Steven had group D and finished seventh.
Taylor had group F and finished first.

From clue 1, the guests with block groups B, D, E, and F finished first, fourth, sixth, and seventh, in some combination. From clue 2, the guests with block groups A, C, D, and G were Brianna, Cheryl, Danny, and Steven, in some combination. From clues 1 and 2 combined, no one among Aria, Kelly, and Taylor finished second, third, or fifth. From clue 3, Kelly also finished neither first nor seventh, and therefore Kelly finished fourth or sixth, Brianna finished third or fifth, and Steven finished fifth, sixth, or seventh.

From clue 4, the guest with block group B did not finish first or seventh, the guest with block group E did not finish first, and the guest with block group F didn't finish sixth or seventh. From clue 6, Aria didn't finish first (since she finished behind Danny) or sixth or seventh (since she finished ahead of group G, who finished fifth at worst), so she finished fourth. That means the guest with group G finished fifth, and Danny finished first, second, or third. By elimination, Kelly finished sixth, so per clue 3, Brianna finished fifth (and had group G) and Steven finished seventh. By elimination, Taylor finished first.

From clue 5, since Kelly finished sixth, the guest with block group D finished seventh, and so Steven had group D. Taylor, the first-place finisher, thus had group F.

Per previous eliminations, Cheryl and Danny, in some combination, were assigned groups A and C and finished second and third. Since Cheryl finished ahead of group A (clue 7), she finished second and had group C, and Danny had group A and finished third. Per clue 4, group B must have finished fourth (and so Aria had that group) and group E was assigned to the sixth-place finisher, Kelly.

Bonus Puzzle

The combinations of guests whose three towers will cause Gordon to lose the game when he goes first are:

Aria, Cheryl, Danny (groups B, C, A)
Danny, Steven, Kelly (groups A, D, E)
Brianna, Danny, Taylor (groups G, A, F)
Aria, Brianna, Steven (groups B, G, D)
Aria, Kelly, Taylor (groups B, E, F)
Brianna, Cheryl, Kelly (groups G, C, E)
Cheryl, Steven, Taylor (groups C, D, F)

Note that each guest is part of three groups that include every other guest once; and so, for example, Aria would divide the guests into the pairs Cheryl–Danny, Brianna–Steven, and Kelly–Taylor to give herself a winning combination of blocks when teamed with any of the three pairs, as long as Gordon makes the first move.

The solution to "All the Marbles" involved writing the values of the three groups of marbles as binary numbers and making a takeaway move that resulted in there being an even number of 1's in each column. In the hypothetical game Gordon discussed in which there were towers of two, three, and four blocks, the numbers of blocks would be written 10, 11, and 100, respectively, in binary. The odd number of 1's in both the 4's and 1's columns can only be eliminated by removing three blocks from the tower of four, leaving 10, 11, and 01, where there are equal numbers of 1's in the 2's and 1's columns. This is a "zero" position in which whoever moves first loses, since a move taking away a 1 from either or both columns can be countered by a move that restores an even number of 1's to each column.

If the towers of blocks were all simple stacks of blocks like groups A and F, the same approach would work here. But how do we determine the value of a group such as B?

One way is to find a simple tower, whose value would be equal to the number of blocks in it, that is equal to the value of group B. If we could find such a tower, then a game played with it and group B should be a game with value zero, in which the first player to move loses.

Since there are four blocks in group B, let's see what happens if we play this game with two towers as shown below: group B (left) and a simple tower of four blocks. The first player can make a move that takes away one, two, three, or all four blocks from the simple tower.

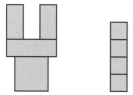

It's obvious that removing all the blocks from the tower on the right would be a losing move, since the second player could do the same with group B by removing its lowest block. Removing three blocks would also fail for the first player, since the second player could remove the block just above the bottom block in group B, leaving just one block.

But suppose the first player only removes two blocks from the simple tower. What move can the second player then make to reduce group B to a value of 2? There is no such move, since removing one of the top blocks leaves a tower of three, and the first player could then just remove the other top block from group B, leaving two towers of two blocks each. Nor would it help the second player to remove one or both blocks from the tower the first player took two blocks from, since the first player can reduce group B to one block or no blocks with one move.

So a tower of two blocks balances group B to create a zero position in which whoever moves next loses. This means that the value of group B is 2.

Now compare Group C to a tower of four blocks.

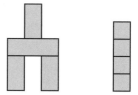

Removing all the blocks from the tower on the right would be a losing move, since the second player could then remove the horizontal block, leaving two single blocks, and the next player to remove a block will lose. Removing three blocks from the tower on the right will also lose, since the second player can remove either of the two "legs" at the bottom to leave a single block. If the first player removes two blocks from the tower, the second player can remove the top block from the group at left to create a winning position (after any next move, it will be possible to reduce the position to two single blocks). But if the first player begins by removing just one block from the tower on the right, the second player will have no winning answer: Removing the top block is answered by removing one more block from the tower, removing the horizontal block is answered by removing the bottom block from the tower on the right, and removing one of the legs of the left group is answered by reducing the tower on the right to a single block. Group C, therefore, is equivalent to a simple tower of three blocks and has a value of 3.

In mathematical terms, such a value in an "impartial" game (a game in which the same moves are available to both players) is referred to as a "nim-value." In one move, as we saw, group B can be reduced to a value of 0, 1, or 3, but not to 2; and in one move, Group C can be reduced to a value of 0, 1, or 2, but not 3. A group's nim-value will always be the lowest whole-number value that cannot be obtained by making a move in that group. (This number is known as the "mex," or minimum excluded value.) For example, with one move group F can be reduced to anywhere from zero to six blocks, so its nim-value is 7. With this in mind, it is easy to determine the values of the other groups, which are as follows: A = 1, B = 2, C = 3, D = 4 (taking away the top block leaves C, which has a value of 3; this technique can also be used to determine the values of E and G), E = 5, F = 7, and G = 6.

Continuing with the approach that worked in "All the Marbles," here are the values of towers A through G written as binary numbers (with some extra zeros put in front of the first three numbers to align all the columns):

A	001
B	010
C	011
D	100
E	101
F	111
G	110

With perfect play, every position in an impartial game is either a win for the first player (who can make a move that brings about a zero position) or a win for the second player (when the position is already a zero position).

By choosing sets of three towers whose values in binary together contain an even number of 1's in each column (when the values are written above one another), you create a zero position in which any first move Gordon can make will create an odd number of 1's in at least one column. Since the way nim-values are determined assures that all lower values can be reached, there will always be a countermove available to restore a zero position.

For further information, read about the Sprague-Grundy theorem in a source such as Wikipedia.

Puzzle 10.5: Endgame

Felix Jr. and Morgan met in Virginia during weekend 3, and so Morgan is the guilty visitor.

Felix visited the states in the order Pennsylvania, Delaware, Virginia, Maryland.
Hugh visited the states in the order Delaware, Maryland, Pennsylvania, Virginia.
John visited the states in the order Virginia, Maryland, Pennsylvania, Delaware.
Morgan visited the states in the order Maryland, Pennsylvania, Virginia, Delaware.
Rachel visited the states in the order Maryland, Pennsylvania, Delaware, Virginia.
Wendy visited the states in the order Delaware, Virginia, Maryland, Pennsylvania.

Clue 4 indicates that Hugh, Morgan, and Wendy were not in Delaware during weekends 2 or 3, and that no two of them were in the same state during one of those weekends. From clues 1 and 5, Felix Jr. and Wendy visited Maryland and Pennsylvania during weekend 4, in some combination. By elimination, the only time Wendy can have visited Delaware is weekend 1.

From clue 6, John was not in Pennsylvania during weekend 1. From clue 7, Rachel was also not in Pennsylvania during weekend 1, nor was she in Virginia that weekend. Since none of the other three visitors were in Pennsylvania during weekend 1 either (clue 3), Felix Jr. was (clue 1), which means that he was not in Pennsylvania during weekend 4, and so Wendy was, and Felix Jr. was in Maryland.

Only John could have visited Virginia during weekend 1 (per previous deductions and the eliminations in clue 3), and so he must have done so. Since he did not visit Virginia in any other weekend, he visited Delaware in week 4. Returning to clue 6, John was in Maryland during weekend 2 and in Pennsylvania during weekend 3.

Only Felix Jr. and Rachel could have visited Delaware during weekends 2 and 3, and so they each were there during one of those weekends, and Rachel was not there during weekends 1 or 4. The only state Rachel could have visited during weekend 1 is therefore Maryland, and the only state she could have visited during weekend 4 was Virginia. From clue 7, she visited Pennsylvania during weekend 2 and Delaware during weekend 3. Felix Jr. therefore visited Delaware during weekend 2 and Virginia during weekend 3.

From clue 8, Hugh was in Maryland during weekend 2, and so neither Morgan nor Wendy was there at that time (clue 4), and Hugh was in Delaware during weekend 1 and therefore in Virginia in weekend 4, leaving Pennsylvania for weekend 3. By elimination, Wendy was in Virginia during weekend 2 and in Maryland during weekend 3. Morgan was therefore not in Maryland or Pennsylvania during weekend 3 (clue 4), and so Morgan was in Virginia at that time. Morgan therefore had to be in Delaware during weekend 4, Maryland during weekend 1, and Pennsylvania during weekend 2.

Late Summer

Ojai Puzzle 2: Arrangements

The correct chronological order of the photos is K, A, C, E, J, F, H, B, L, I, D, G.

Gordon's and Taylor's guesses ranged from two below to two more than the correct answer, and other numbers can be excluded. Nina's ranged from two below to three above the correct numbers, and other numbers can be excluded. Comparing the lists of remaining possible numbers based on the three sets of guesses and excluding any numbers that are not possible for all three guesses yields these possibilities:

A	3, 2, 1
B	9, 8, 7
C	4, 3, 2
D	12, 11, 10, 9
E	5, 4, 3
F	6
G	12, 11, 10
H	8, 7, 6
I	10
J	6, 5, 4
K	3, 2, 1
L	9

The 6's, 9's, and 10's for photos other than F, I, and L can be ignored.

Nina's guess of 9 for F accounts for her guess three higher than the correct answer, and her guess of 8 for I accounts for her guess two below the correct answer. Accordingly, these additional possibilities can be ruled out: 2 for C, 5 for E, 8 for H, and 3 for K. By elimination, H is 7 and B is 8. Also, J is now the only possibility for 5.

Since only A and K can be 1 or 2, they must be these numbers in some combination.

Taylor's three correct guesses can only be D, E, and K, and so D is 11, E is 4, and K is 1. By elimination, A is 2, C is 3, and G is 12.

Also Available

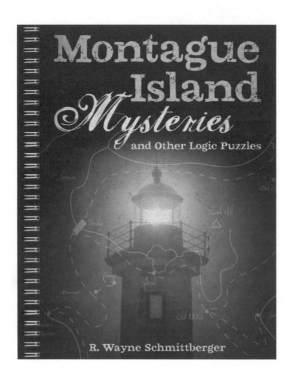

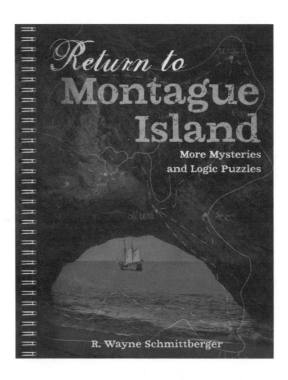